The Essentials of Being

Pam Wade ND Ph.D.
Rhonda Etherton MS. DD.

CONTENTS

Section One

Section Two

The Essentials of Being is a reference to understanding the 12 energies that move through us all. It details the facets of those energies—including names, colors, and sounds—that combine to help balance your centers. These facets are further expanded in a collection of original music, *Songs of the Chakras*, and a line of Bath and Body Nutrients.

Songs of the Chakras aids in balance, restores peace and is good for sleeping, calming, and aligning your 12 centers while each corresponding Bath and Body Nutrient feeds your system and helps release imbalance. Some examples include Auto Immune, Fibromyalgia, Restless Leg, Blood, Blood Sugar, Female/Male Issues, Joints, Mood Lifter, Digestion, and Sleep.

We are all unique and beautiful. However, if you find you are a Ni-mahn/Cal-mahr, Cal-mahr/Ni-mahn, or Tol-mahr/Re-ah, you are extra sensitive with deep feelings—especially boys growing into men who are taught to suck it up and not show emotions.

Often families are born with the same combinations of energy centers to assist one another in their soul's growth. Understanding your child's energy centers will help you understand and guide them to be their very best. They already know it, if you don't teach them to fit in *your* box. Let them know how special they are and to trust their feelings. Listen to them. They have much to share with you.

"The Essentials of Being" will take you to wisdoms within the deepest part of your being.

Your divine I AM presence will dissolve any uncertainty with whom you are and what you are here to experience. You will have an understanding of your relationships within your family ties and how you are contributing to your life experience together.

Learning the 12 energy centers helps you to tune into your divine network. It is a knowingness that goes beyond words. Your spirit comes alive and remembers who you really are. Your spirit has guided you across all time, space and dimensions to people and events to help you remember how beautiful and powerful you really are. Your mission is to believe and awaken to the God I AM, as you uncover and remember your divine true self.

Your divine self has been challenging you all along to embrace life with your heart, not just the mind. Through millennium it was discovered the mind doesn't hold all the answers. It has been compartmentalizing events and strategizing actions to get what you want from the ego (the little mind).

This book will help you to see your true self and illumine the places within your field of energy so you may choose with your heart (spirit) and higher wisdom, rather than choosing from fear (ego). I believe this to be the quote from the Bible, when Jesus speaks *You cannot serve two masters*—Fear and Love.

When making decisions for yourself, know from which you choose, Fear or Love?

Living from the heart, which is your divine spirit, is what holds the key to your true wisdom. 60,000 years have come and gone with great divine beings working in love to assist us with awakening this planet to our divinity. Their teachings have awakened the heart of humanity and helped us know that the heart of all of creation is available to move through us and help assist in creating a magnificent life. The purpose was and still is to help us remember we are co-creators with our Heavenly Mother and Father God.

The "Essentials of Being" will bring about change. Learning the divine spiritual nature of the 12 energy centers will bring enlightenment to the very core of your existence.

The Hal-lai Healing System calls forth your divine light. When we separated from our source of light into human beings, it was foretold that humanity must learn about individual ego so it can become illumined and purified back into the light.

My dear friend and colleague Rev. Pam Wade agreed to facilitate this book for Hal-lai. Her service to humanity will always be remembered by many. The collection of wisdom contained within this book is from sacred knowledge passed on for the purpose of the souls enlightenment.

We are the strongest of the strong to be alive during this time of transformation into this 7th Golden Era. Our cells know it and our divine blueprint is transforming into it. You came to bring about change. If you are reading these words then I hope your heart will be touched and you will become an unmovable, unshakable light upon your path. It is time to pick up your staff of power!

With gratitude I thank you, thank you beloved Machia, your divine teachings have helped me to understand light and divine timing. To our beloved Ascended Masters, Council of Golden Light and the Beings of Light for your endless service of love and devotion to our little planet called Earth.

Much Love,

Rhonda Etherton

First and foremost I acknowledge the Spirit which resides not only in the heart of all creation but also within the heart of all beings. For that source of Love is the driving force behind the creation of this book and it is to that source I first submit its contents.

I also recognize and acknowledge the Love of the Creator manifesting through human embodiment. The love and support of my Life Partner offered through many hours of pouring over proofs and listening to my ramblings. You gave me the courage to continue and keep my perspective on the important things of life. Thank you for those ever present and all important questions that assisted me in returning my focus to presenting a clearer understanding, and reminding me not to take myself too seriously. Now and forever I owe you my being.

To so many of my friends, seen and unseen, that have assisted me through growth and supported me through the darkest of dark I owe the strength and happiness I have become.

Pam Wade

The Essentials of Being calls the reader to expand their understanding of the illumination of the soul and spirituality. It is designed to assist the reader in finding balance in their life physically, mentally, emotionally, and spiritually.

The information is based in the text of the Bible, Human Anatomy, Atlantian legend, Eastern Philosophy, Spirituality, and inspired wisdom presented through the author. You are challenged to utilize your own inner knowing as you read and apply the knowledge offered.

This book offers possibilities based in fact, history, faith, and soul remembrance and is designed to awaken within you the ability to become whole.

The Essentials of Being is a reference for two powerful healing modalities: Hal-lái Bath and Body Nutrients and Levite Stone Treatment. Both of these modalities are designed to awaken the individual to recognize their own perfection and innate healing ability. Innate abilities are those that we possess within us but are often latent and not recognized. These modalities also assist the individual in increasing the effectiveness of their work toward illumination.

The book is presented in two sections. Section One presents background information on each of the Essentials, and Biblical text in an expanded understanding of traditional presentation. They are presented in a manner to challenge the reader's understanding and offers a foundation upon which to build the stepping stones of Section Two.

On page 79 you will find a diagram which we call "The Essential Being" illustrating the location of each Essential in relation to the physical body. Section Two contains a quick reference page on each of the 12 Essentials and the manner in which the reader can utilize them to blend the physical, mental, emotional, and spiritual into a whole and balanced being.

The title Essential is utilized because each one is necessary or essential to becoming a being that is blended with:

- Sustaining the physical body in its highest level of health; free from disease and limitation
- Maintaining mental and emotional health, joy, and peace
- Opening the heart and mind to recognize the potential and power of the indwelling spirit
- Receiving and utilizing Divine guidance and direction
- Utilizing all that is available to manifest, all that is possible
- Returning to the awareness that we are masters of not only our own destiny but that of the world
- Becoming responsible co-creators in our future

When an individual becomes a truly blended being they no longer are subject to the power of fear. They have learned and can in an instant access the skills, emotions, words, and actions necessary to remove anger, doubt, and hesitation. Fully blended individuals make wise choices that lead to establishing love, joy, and peace in their lives.

As we progress toward this goal we will find ourselves revisiting aspects of each of the Essentials. This is common. Clearing and balancing one level of an Essential often exposes another level in need of balance. Don't become impatient or harsh with yourself, it is all part of your growth. Continue forward, it is a worthy goal. Keep working. Keep growing. Use all of the modalities available to you. You are worth it and all of creation needs you whole and complete.

SECTION ONE

CHAPTER ONE

In the Beginning

A great novel once began; "It was the best of times, it was the worst of times..." And so it is for our age. We have behind us the great learning experiences of war, peace, chaos, confusion and the teachings offered to us by many masters. Some of whose writings and letters are collected in the Bible. We have before us war, chaos, confusion and the great learning experiences promised by many prophets. Upon us lies the opportunity for understanding. Understanding of the promise of enlightenment, healing, and unity of spirit through the simple path whereon we stand.

The Old Testament has given us a chronicle and the New Testament has given us a path. Now through The Spirit of Truth is given a way, The Essentials of Being. A way to understand, heal, walk in light and love, balanced and in peace. Peace, not as the world gives, but as is given from The Counselor, whom The Father will send in my name, who will teach you all things, and bring to your remembrance all that I have said to you (John 14:26).

It is time for us to have understanding of things to come. It is time for us to have understanding of the way our thoughts, words and deeds contribute to the world conditions and our own personal health. This we cannot do if we continue to accept another individual's interpretation and do not accept responsibility for our own physical body and growth of our spirit. We must understand the Essentials of our own being and the spirit that dwells within to enable us to bring about enlightened change.

Much of what you will read is your history because it is the history upon which the beliefs and energy of the Earth is built. What you are being asked to do is recognize the part of you that continues to exist in that past and create the change that will allow you to step out of that history and begin to exist in the moment and empower your future.

What does empowering mean? To empower yourself you must place the full energy of your mind, body and spirit into recognizing your potential and your ability to act upon it. The power to bring about healing, balance, and the fullness of your potential lies within you. Sometimes we just need the outward stimulation and recognition to be able to see it within.

If we come to a point in our lives where we no longer feel, it only takes someone hurting us to again awaken the ability to respond. Often times it takes an external stimulation to produce an internal response. Whether it is through the use of words of validation from another or the production of desired results doesn't matter. As long as we awaken to the truth that we had it all along we are becoming empowered. Wherever you place your faith it will grow. Wherever you grow you become empowered.

So then if it is necessary to utilize; tones, affirmations, oils, medical or natural treatments, and other forms of stimulation to awaken our ability to respond from within then let us do so with joy. Joy that someone was inspired to develop them. Joy that they are available to us as tools to begin the building. Joy that we have the wisdom to make ourselves strong. The more physical senses you fill the faster your progress.

The twelve Essentials are energy systems that, when operating properly, empower your life positively to bring about change. They are not physical organs or body systems but they do correlate to them. They are the energy system that empowers not only the body but also the mind and spirit to function as designed. Much like the outlet in your wall that empowers your appliances.

Just as passion and desire empower you to act in a certain manner to accomplish a goal, so the twelve Essentials provide the ability. The heart is not the only place that the life force of blood exists but it is the heart that empowers it to flow through the rest of the body.

CHAPTER TWO

The Need for Understanding

It is sometimes difficult to express or convey techniques to bring yourself into a state of balance. For what you are working with in the twelve Essentials is energy. It is not concrete. It is not something that you can see with the naked eye or hold tightly within your grasp. In order to achieve a balanced state of health, mental clarity, emotional stability, prosperity, and peace that comes with balance you will be asked to consider abstract concepts.

The degree that these concepts are abstract is measured by the level of acceptance you have for everyday tasks and occurrences. When you awake in the morning and want to know how to dress for the day based on the weather, you simply pick up a remote, press a button, and the information becomes available. You accept that the television knows which frequencies to pick out of the atmosphere surrounding you to bring you that information. When you glance at your watch to know where you need to be, you accept that its intricate workings are in harmony with others and you will be on time. When you walk into your home late at night you do not have to consider the mechanics of electricity to be able to flip a switch and illumine the room. During sleep you do not give conscious thought to your breathing or the beating of your heart, but they continue. So much of our daily existence is based in the acceptance of the creations of the hands and minds of humankind without consideration to how it is brought into being.

We are discovering more about the human body daily; how it is constructed, how it works, and how to repair it. The difficult understanding is why it works and how it came into being. This is left to abstract thinking. What causes us to have different personalities, opinions, levels of intelligence, likes and dislikes, humors, and appearances are still studied and examined by science. The results of these studies present facts that we can accept because they are measurable and proven.

Energy is known to exist. It is measurable. It is proven. The Essentials that we will be working with consist of energy. This energy does not take a physically distinguishable form but it does create measurable results. It reacts to our choices in much the same manner as tuning in to a television station.

Choosing a specific channel produces a sought after presentation on the screen. If you no longer want to take part in the energy pattern displayed, you choose differently and a different pattern is displayed. When the program no longer brings you joy you can select a different program. Life doesn't offer us the convenience of a remote control but the ability to recognize and produce what we desire is the control in our hands.

The energy of the twelve Essentials is much like the availability of the channels we take for granted on our televisions. As we begin to learn the different programming we can start the process of adjusting our reception until we produce the desired results. Once we clear up the interference we begin to enjoy the clarity of the picture and choose what we will bring into our life.

The twelve Essentials of your being are much like the primary networks available on your television. Each one has a specific frequency that it operates on and programming that is unique. Bringing the Essentials into balance is like adjusting the alignment of an antenna to ensure you receive the clearest and strongest signal. When the alignment is correct the signal is strong and the programming operates at its maximum potential.

When a new program is offered all we need to know is the time and channel and we can align the television to receive the energy that it has to offer. In much the same manner we can utilize the energy of the twelve Essentials to receive what life has to offer. It is not necessary for us to understand how the television produces what we seek. That understanding we are willing to leave to the wisdom of its creators. It is only necessary that we:

- Acquire the receiver (our body)
- Tap into a source of power (our Essentials)
- Use it in the manner it was designed by the inventor (our Creator)
- Select a channel (choose)
- Change the channel when we are no longer happy (choose again)
- Obtain a clear result (balance)

Just as different areas offer different and unique availability of programs, different individuals have unique levels of balance. The one constant in all operating televisions is they have the same potential to access everything offered. The one constant in every living being is that we all have the ability to access everything that is our potential.

If you understand all the features of your television equipment, you can greatly increase your joy by utilizing all of its options. The more you learn about and use its resources, the easier it becomes to recreate the results you desire. With practice you learn how to replace worn out batteries. You discover how to control the volume, adjust the quality of color, focus, brightness, and continue through each feature until you achieve satisfaction.

The twelve Essentials of your being are a concept which is no more abstract than turning on the news every morning. When you understand the features and learn how to utilize the energy, you will tune in to the desired results. We trust that a creation of humankind will function in a desired manner. We should anticipate no less from a Divine creation.

When your television is not operating properly you notice difficulties and take it in for repair. When the twelve Essentials are not in balance they also produce noticeable difficulties and need assistance to return to proper functioning.

Just as a technician has the diagnostics and tools to adjust and fine tune your set, they also exist to adjust the Essentials. The greatest difference is that when your television reaches a certain point the technician no longer has the ability to repair it and you must replace it. It is no longer worth the expense or labor. Your life and well being are always worth the work. The technician of your life, you, always have what you need and the only price is the desire and commitment to return to your perfection.

Being happy, loved, and abundant in all areas of your life is achievable. What is required is that you make every effort to do the best you are capable of doing. If you are not seeing the desired results in your life, evaluate your participation and make change where it is necessary.

If you feel that circumstances and people prohibit you from positive change consider that they only control you if your choices allow them to. If you don't like the results of your choices, choose again. Change the channel utilizing the wisdom of your program guide, the Essentials of your being. You have the source of power; you only need the understanding of how to use it. The controls are in the understanding; the remote is in your hands. Another can only control your life if you hand it over to them.

Take charge of your choices and act upon them. Take charge of your life and live it fully. It is essential to your being.

CHAPTER THREE

If So Then...

We have many roads which move across the face of the Earth. When we have traveled different roads, we understand that they are all part of a greater system. They all have the same objective, to assist us in moving from one point to the next and take us from our departure point to our destination.

The path of the 12 Essentials of Being which follows is designed in the same manner as a map. They are avenues for us to explore and discover for ourselves individually. Some roads will lead us to our destination more quickly; some will lead us on a more colorful winding way.

We are the holders of the map. We choose the roads upon which to travel. We make our own selections of the stopping points and times of arrival. We pick the time and length of rest. We may encounter many others along the way and oftentimes travel together sharing stories experiences and love. All of them become a part of us. We can take a snapshot of points in our journey, but we can never return to them. We continue forward; forward upon the road that brings us home and no matter how long our absence the warmth of love awaits us and the companionship of the Spirit of the journey embraces us.

You build within yourself remembrances of your journey that become the most precious part of your life that unites you to each other and to the memory of love. This love is unconditional, all embracing, ever empowering and ever waiting. This love is where the journey begins and also where it will end.

This is the same love that we continue to seek throughout our lives. It is a strong and relentless fuel that propels us along the diversified directions that we take. Every stop we make we do so in the hope of reuniting ourselves with that remembrance of love that dwells within us. We constantly run into detours and obstructions, forgetting the importance of the sharing of that love and hoping to accumulate it in case we need it down the road.

So then we travel further. So then we travel longer and take the road that presents itself and strive to incorporate all of the fullness of life. We open ourselves to endless and unlimited experiences interacting with countless other lives. We seek to find ourselves but fail to recognize our reflection in the eyes of others.

Until we can truly understand our departure point and where we exist within it we cannot plan a route to our destination. Until we recognize where love exists within our own being and open ourselves to the very essentials of our being we cannot begin. We must prepare the vehicle of our soul and lighten the load of our doubts and fears to enable us to empower ourselves with the ability to make the journey.

We must carry only the necessary supplies the Essentials of our being. We must bring ourselves to a point of recognition that there is nothing to fear in the construction of our vehicle or the way it has been prepared for the journey. We must trust that it will carry us over the mountains and through the valley of the shadow of death until we remember that we control the trip and love will lead us home, together.

You have awaiting you now the 12 Essentials of your being. These concepts are the centers for your discovery, utilization and implementation. It is our hope that the Essentials given within this text can offer you understanding and guidance for their incorporation. You may find upon your journey that the internalization of these Essentials becomes a process of building within yourself and a sharing of the road with all of us who search for solutions and answers. Answers to questions that have burned deeply within each of us. Questions that have remained unanswered because we continue to seek solutions outside of our own connection to the Essentials of our being.

You have here a foundation. The Essentials of your being. You are the carpenters, you are the builders, and you are the architects. The foundation is laid. It is offered but without your participation in awakening these Essentials within yourself, there is no building. There is only a foundation.

But upon this foundation stand pillars of wisdom. Pillars of wisdom to use as your guideposts to set strongly into your development, healing, knowledge and growth.

Chapter Four

Experience

Our lives are unique learning processes of opportunities that each of us is allowed to experience in our own manner. For not only can we individually experience opportunities, we have the ability to learn from another. Then, all of us do not have to experience the entire life journey in all of the manners available. If one chooses to experience a life path in one manner then we can learn from them and no longer have the need for that life experience. You can choose to learn by observing or you can choose to learn by experience. In either manner the importance lies in the depth of wisdom gained. Do we watch and often times assist another through an experience only to repeat the same actions and reactions? Or, do we gain wisdom from their experience and grow with that individual?

It is a wonderful, flexible quality that we as individuals possess. The ability to be aware of wise choices when another walks through life opportunities. It is a difficult quality to exhibit when we open the door to the same opportunity.

We have been given many opportunities to learn by observing through the past. So often though we cannot internalize an experience until such time that we experience it for ourselves. It is not necessary though for one individual to experience everything in creation. If you are building a house, there are some who come and lay the foundation. There are some who build the frame. There are some that install electricity and others who install water. The house is still built whether by one or by many. Now, if we hope that we do not have to experience any learning opportunities and only learn by observing, then we become as the subcontractor. We become responsible for the outcome of everything.

Just like a strand of Christmas lights, all are independent light, but yet connected to each and plugged into the same energy source. Each time you have an experience, thought, action or even breath or heartbeat, it empowers the light within you. It then follows the strand back to the source and all lights become brighter. For when a friend is going through a rough stage in their life, it is always more clear to you what is happening to them. You wish you could help them. You wish you could take the experience over for them or change it. The reason you can feel it, see it and understand it is because their light is flickering and the flow of the experience is passing through you also. You are becoming more enlightened because of that friend's experience and the whole is becoming stronger. So, then thank your friend for allowing you to be a part of their experience and allowing you to learn from it. Then learn and move forward with clarity. You cannot make an experience stop, for then the whole does not learn. The wonderful experiences of life are the easiest to learn but never forget to be grateful for the opportunity to share them. These experiences can lift you out of the darkness and because of another's joy; you can be catapulted into light. So then, seek the love and joy in all experiences and be instrumental in uplifting the whole.

This sharing of experience is why it is inappropriate to try and change another, to save them. This is why it is so important to learn together and assist one another so that we may learn from each other's experience and be the keeper of wisdom for one another. Keeping wisdom learned through experience so it may be shared builds a strong foundation and answers positively to the question, "Am I my brother's keeper?" (Genesis 4:9)

CHAPTER FIVE

God as our Being

Before you begin to balance and awaken the Essentials of your being, we challenge you to expand your perception of God. Consider the moment of the decision to separate the wholeness of God and become products of creation. If God is our beginning, and we are born of Him, then just as our own conception of a child we are an active and growing part of His being.

While we are still in that womb, or wholeness of God before creation, we are aware of the choices that are being made that will effect our life experience and set in motion our existence. Just as a child within your own body reacts to choices that you make. We then in that moment when we were completely one and not separate from God were aware of what was being created for us. Just as a child within the womb reacts to the way you treat your body we actively participate in the creation.

For before there was God personified there was "the Spirit of God." (Genesis 1:2) Before God created man and woman God was not alone for it is written, "Let us make man in our image, after our likeness." (Genesis 1:26) In Genesis 1, it is written that God created man and woman but not until Genesis 2 does God create Adam and subsequently Eve. So if we are then all a product of God's creation then at some point we were all a part of God awake and aware of the full thought of creation.

We are told that much of our religion and spiritual belief is to be accepted on faith. Faith often becomes a measuring rod. If someone prays for something and receives it then their faith was strong. If they pray for healing and are not healed then their faith was weak. What if faith is truly as simple as the mustard seed and is the releasing of doubt and fear? Possibly then faith is Fear Absent In The Heart.

Possibly then we need to expand our concept of God.

Consider the moment of the decision to create and separate from the oneness of God. The oneness where all hearts, all minds and all beings were complete in God. In that wholeness came the decision to create or invest the whole with a new form. Then came the collective decision "Let us make . . ." to separate from that. In that remaining portion, that part which continued the creative process, a part of you still remains. No more than your child can ever cease to be a part of you or you cease to be a part of them can you be separated from that part which we define as God.

Let us attempt an illustration of God. If each was to choose two pieces from a pile of colored glass to represent ourselves we could begin. In your choosing you are allowed to pick one of any color but the second one has to be green. Then everyone has one green colored glass and one that is different. In using pieces of glass as representations of ourselves, we need to note that they are transparent and therefore reflect the quality of God. This is the quality of God that has no physical substance and is love. Then you place your glass piece, which is different into a central pile. In this central pile all have placed their piece of a different color. In that pile would be a Gathering Of Diversities, where each and every one has a unique, individualized part. Since some of them are the same color, it might be difficult for you to relocate your own individual piece. This might divide you into groups or races seeking your part in your way, which is unified by obvious similarity.

Now even in the mixing of these pieces each individual has a part in the central pile and each one has one left. One aspect of your being will be taken from within that central mind and enter into an earthly experience to teach, to learn, to grow. This is the part that keeps trying to build a path to return. This is your active part of creation, remembering from whence you came and working to return. That is the piece of glass that you still hold in your hands, your individualized expression. The green one is the fragile, transparent, many faceted and reflective piece of the creative process. But, the constant of your being which is always with GOD and goes to rejoin God will be left. Therefore, the whole is a part of its collective pieces and more than any one part.

This is why we place the concept of God as a deity, a guiding force because it contains not only a part of you but also a part of all knowledge and wisdom. It contains a part of yourself that you no longer recognize within yourself or others and a part of others that you fail to see.

We are told that God is light as revealed in the words of John. If we then look to Revelation 22:13 we also find "I am the Alpha and the Omega, the first and the last, the beginning and the end." From this we can feel assured that from light we came and to light we will return. A return that can occur when we remove our focus from the darkness of our mental creation and place it back upon the light of our spirit. God is that point from which we began, exist as our diversified beings, and return.

When you move into a new awareness of God and cease to feel separateness from God you may open your awareness to the blending of God. You are then not limiting yourself to "I am here, God is there." There is no longer a need to try to perceive God separate from yourself. When you move into that blended awareness you may then begin to open yourself and the dwelling place of God which is within your own being. You are no longer separate from God, God dwells within you and you may begin to work with His Essentials of Being. As stated "For we are the temple of the living God; as God said, 'I will live in them and move among them.'" (2 Corinthians 6:16)

CHAPTER SIX

Wisdom vs. Knowledge

We are in a time where there is a necessity for an acceleration of learning. Acceleration in the increase of wisdom can then occur. As you expand your awareness and open yourself to all possibilities and all probabilities, you continue to remove your fears of the same. You may then come to a point of recognizing assistance. Assistance offered by the spirit speeds your acquiring of wisdom.

You need to acquire wisdom. Knowledge is important but it serves no purpose if it is not utilized. Just as was the prayer of Paul for the Ephesians; "That the Father of glory, may give you a spirit of wisdom and of revelation in the knowledge of him, having the eyes of your heart enlightened, that you may know what is the hope to which he has called you," (Ephesians 1:17, 18). Therefore, as Paul recognized, wisdom comes from the revelation of knowledge. The ability to see and utilize knowledge creates wisdom.

What purpose would it serve you to understand how a spacecraft is powered? In your life, as it now exists, that would probably not serve a purpose for you. Therefore, that is knowledge. What is wished to be shared is wisdom. For this is what the Earth is in need of. What occurs so often in societies is that those who have wisdom are also those who are least heard.

As you gain wisdom you are increasing it for the entire Earth. For wisdom is knowledge empowered by experience and application. As you look upon that which you think you want to know, look also upon that which has been known. It is often called Ancient Wisdom but it is ever as important as current wisdom. There are many ancient wisdoms that have long awaited application and now seem new to those who seek solutions and answers for their hungry spirit.

It is a very necessary part of the process that the Earth is going through to expand that wisdom. In your expansion of your own wisdom you increase the speed or intensity of which Earth can change toward a brighter future. All of the knowledge of all of creation awaits and is not just for a select few. That knowledge is for those who wish it as they, "Ask, and it will be given you; seek and you will find; knock, and it will be opened to you" (Matthew 7:7).

All it requires is that you prepare yourself and open your heart and spirit to receive. For when you prepare and wait and ask with the intent for the highest good of all, the Spirit of Truth will come to you and reveal to you all that is necessary for the continuance of growth and the opening into the Essentials of your Being.

CHAPTER SEVEN

Intent

Intent can create or destroy everything. Intent is the power by which you live upon this Earth. Intent is the energy that drives this Earth. It is why you are; it is your life force.

Intent is the focusing of your energy. The energy of your actions and thoughts follow your intent just as the archer drawing back the arrow, with proper focus. The arrow follows the intent to hit the target. That same energy can remove your focus away from your intent when you allow yourself to be overcome by emotion. Feelings of inadequacies and lack do not as often arise within you if the intent remains constant.

If you dwell in the energy of sadness, even when you are intent upon being joyful, you are placing so much of your energy into the sadness that you do not have the ability to focus back to your intent. If you can keep your eyes and heart directed in the path of your intent all things will follow.

So often the heart believes fully in what you are doing and how you are doing it. Then you allow other thoughts and fears to cloud that belief. Very often you do not even realize that it has happened. If you wish to achieve something you may be fearful that the amount of time, money and energy you will need to invest may not be returned to you. That small, hidden fear has the ability to cloud the entire intent and you become so involved in your fear that you cannot focus your intent. You cannot focus your energy to pursue anything.

When an emergency arises, it is easier to focus your energy and intent. Your body will even respond with the producing of adrenaline and you are capable of performing tremendous feats. If you can learn through focusing your intent and energy, to activate that same response, you can accomplish anything. If you are attempting to move an extremely heavy object and you keep pulling and pulling and it suddenly breaks free, you can then continue to move with that object. This is possible because you are so extremely focused upon your intent that all available energy works with you, for your intent was good. If you lose focus in the middle of the task though you find that you must begin again. When you have accomplished a task in this manner there is not a need for acclaim or recognition, you feel good about yourself and are content with your actions.

If you look closely enough and deeply enough you will find in a lack of desire (the not wanting to do, or learn) a fear which is the root of it. Oftentimes, it is a fear that you cannot do or understand. Additionally, you often fear that you will not do it well enough. This fear manifests itself in a lack of desire or motivation.

Intent works through the heart. The mind cannot become clear on any objective unless the heart comes into harmony with it. When you make up your mind to do something you sometimes still find it to be difficult to complete the task unless you put all of yourself into it. All of yourself must include the driving force of your being, the heart.

Every time you allow fear to manifest itself through you, you allow your intent to become pulled from its objective. For your heart shadows itself when fear looms imminent. If for one moment while you are moving the heavy object you become fearful that you cannot accomplish it or that you may drop it, your focus and energy is removed from the task and placed into the fear. Therefore, the task remains undone or the object of your focus dropped. Do not feel that you have to use the energy of your intent as power over anything. Use the energy to carry you through the task and onward. Move through that fear, through that task and onward into the next.

Speaking a word in anger takes energy, for anger will be returned to you and you then react by feeling the need to create more anger. Speaking a word in love returns to you love and empowers your driving force through the contentment and wholeness you feel. So then, if fear manifests through anger, hatred, bigotry or any other form it may manifest, it takes control of your intent. When you allow fear to take control, then into fear, you will be plummeted.

Now it is time to begin the process of learning to balance and clear the Essentials of your Being so that you may achieve balance and healing. Now it is time to begin to recognize and utilize all that is available to you to live in health, prosperity, and the fullness of your potential. You enter this process empowered with knowledge. What you must supply is the desire. You have to desire joy. You have to desire utilizing your life to its fullest capacity. You have to desire change within your life that lifts you from the limitations of your past and takes you into the freedom of your future.

The choice is yours. But if you so choose then enter into the discovery of the Essentials and begin the glorious journey into the person you are known to be.

CHAPTER EIGHT

Ei-ahn

Since the beginning of the earthly experience it has been necessary for us to maintain a connection to the Earth. We are fed by her fruits. Her plants provide us with the very air we breathe. Her waters sustain our life and quench our thirst. As we begin the process of returning ourselves to balance, we must begin by bringing ourselves back into harmony with the Earth.

The Earth is not just an accumulation of the things that exist upon it and within it. More importantly, it is an accumulation of the energy of the life experience. Things that grow upon the Earth are well rooted within it. If we desire to have the fullest possible growth from a life experience, then we too must activate the energy of Ei-ahn which deeply roots our spirit into the Earth.

As the unfolding and healing process begins we must first recognize that we are spirit. A spirit encased in a physical body having an earthly experience. As spirit we enter into the body in order to gain wisdom that can only be acquired through the opportunities that life presents us. Our true self or spirit contains the knowledge of our existence as a part of God.

When we begin to access and awaken the energy of Ei-ahn we begin to bring that knowledge into our experiences. How does that awareness assist us in everyday life? How does it enrich life and create balance? Why do we need the power of the Earth blended into an awareness of a spiritual existence?

When Ei-ahn is operating in balance in our lives we begin to consider how our choices will affect the world around us. We recognize that choosing a car that uses a lot of gas results not only in a larger fuel bill but also the depletion of our natural resources. We begin to make choices that result in conserving the Earth before our choices create situations that become worldwide. Choices that create impending disasters such as the Greenhouse effect. This can only be accomplished when our spirit, which is energy, flows fully through us and into the Earth. With our spirit thus rooted we can allow it to begin to fill and influence our thoughts and subsequent actions.

We must realize that the Earth is energy. How else would that which occurs within and upon it naturally sustain and power; our body, our vehicles, heat and cool our homes, and provide all that we need to create dwellings and all that we desire. If the Earth is energy, then we must also presume that it contains a spirit. That spirit is what we begin to understand when we integrate the energy of Ei-ahn into our life.

Because the Earth gives us food, water, shelter, and a place to learn and grow, it is identified as feminine. Being that feminine energy it nurtures us and offers us the opportunity to learn how to nurture others.

The energy of God is most often identified as masculine. That energy is where our spirit begins its journey.

When we are able to allow our spirit to move fully through all of our existence it becomes anchored into the Earth through Ei-ahn. We then blend the masculine and feminine energies and begin to create. Through recognizing this ability to create we gain clearer understanding of how acting on our choices by word, thought, or deed produces consequences. It is by allowing ourselves to view these results from a sense of responsibility that we gain wisdom and give birth to new and more positive opportunities.

A young child looks upon the Earth as a beautiful, magical playground. The Earth herself will teach and discipline the child to respect that which creates pain to the self or another and work along side of that which creates joy. When people shift their focus from that simple awareness and no longer respect the Earth or each other they become imprisoned in their own desires and isolated in their existence.

Through the energy of Ei-ahn the individual may learn how to work successfully with the earth and all that inhabit it. When Ei-ahn is an active energy in our lives and our world there will be an end to wars, anger, hatred, and bigotry. We will all know the value of another and ourselves and do or say nothing that would injure or harm.

Planting a tree, placing your hands within the earth, walking in nature, and performing random acts of kindness are all techniques that assist in integrating the power of Ei-ahn into your life.

The essential oil *Abies Alba* moves through your senses to awaken you to Ei-ahn's existence and clear the obstacles of physical, mental, and emotional toxins that distance you from fully utilizing its energy.

The speed at which Ei-ahn vibrates is the same as the musical note of middle C#. Utilizing that tone calls the sense of hearing into experiencing Ei-ahn's energy and increases the body's ability to recognize its positive potential.

CHAPTER NINE

Re-ah

The basis of most of our beliefs begins in the experiences of our family and cultural past. Stepping out of these patterns they create within us and into new and exciting possibilities takes great courage. You can begin to find the ability within yourself to create a new life and independent thinking by awakening the energy of Re-ah.

Until we gain wisdom through our own life experiences we react to the world through the thoughts of others ingrained into us. If your parents don't like or are afraid of dogs until you experience a dog yourself, you will most likely hold the same fear or aversion. You may miss out on a potentially joyous experience and not even be aware of why. If your culture is bigoted toward another race you may not get acquainted with the one person that could most positively impact your life.

The power of unconditional, non judgmental love resides in Re-ah. It teaches us to make choices based on our experiences with the world instead of a stereotyped conception.

An accessing of this Essential allows us a freedom to grow beyond the level of our environment and entertain the possibility of a more positive future. Individuals who overcome the odds are capable of reaching deep within and utilizing the power of Re-ah. When we observe these people we often think that they have been blessed or have more than average ability. What they are doing is recognizing the energy of Re-ah and utilizing it in making wise choices that carry them into a different reality. A world of their own creation built upon wise, independent choice, not what statistics or society would have them believe.

Re-ah contains the knowledge of our deeper roots; the wisdom of our existence prior to our current life experience. When we release that wisdom we recognize that our spirit is energy and cannot be destroyed. Energy can be changed in form but it cannot be totally eradicated.

If you cut down a tree to build a table, the form of that tree may be gone but its energy has been transformed into a table. The energy of the roots that once fed it becomes part of the earth and part of other plants assisting them in their growth. The stump becomes a shelter and food source for insects; becoming part of their life energy. The table may eventually serve its purpose and be burned. The energy of that portion of the tree is now transformed into heat, smoke, and ash. The heat blends with the air. The smoke rises to the clouds. The ash becomes again a part of the earth that sustained the tree. The tree has been transformed, spread further, but it still exists. So it is with our spirit and Re-ah holds that secret. The secret that allows us to know that we may be transformed from a physical body but our spirit will continue on in a different form.

Not only does Re-ah contain pre-life memory, it is the storehouse for the positive experiences of infancy and early childhood. When you feel joy or love in these years prior to cognitive memory, it is blended into Re-ah's energy and available for reference in the future. When you are placed in situations that require you to make choices, awaken the energy of Re-ah to gain clarity as to which ones will bring you joy. Being fully blended with this Essential creates the ability to clearly see which options awaken the remembrance of joy so that options that create pain or fear are not empowered. This allows you to recognize fear-based reactions and turn them into positive action.

Within Re-ah dwells that part of your being which is unmovable and unshakable. It is not an energy which demands or believes that you are always correct in every circumstance. It is a force that allows you to recognize what is right for the most positive expression of your being without harming another. When in harmony with Re-ah it gives you the capability to be strong like a willow rooted within the earth, able to bend with the winds of change.

This force awakens you to remain in your ability to continue creating in a positive manner, undaunted by what others would have you believe or become. When the energy of Re-ah is utilized without being balanced, its force can consume many individuals. When this occurs, they become someone who must be right in any circumstance and win at any cost.

Recognize the things that bring joy into your life and recreate that feeling in everything you do. Learning how to incorporate enough playtime into your work greatly enhances the utilization of Re-ah's energy. A simple changing of your words from "I have to," to "I get to," and "I should," to "I can," is a powerful beginning to awaken this Essential.

The essential oil *Pelargonium Graveolens* moves through your senses to awaken you to Re-ah's existence and clears the obstacles of physical, mental, and emotional toxins that distance you from fully utilizing its energy.

The speed at which Re-ah vibrates is the same as the musical note of D. Utilizing that tone calls the sense of hearing into experiencing Re-ah's energy and increases the body's ability to recognize its positive potential.

CHAPTER TEN

Si-ah

When negative thoughts begin to rise within you decisions become reactive, made in haste, and without clear consideration. With Si-ah awakened, you have the ability to filter through thoughts and feelings and distinguish which ones are true and which ones are false. You then are motivated by this Essential to discard any concerns or emotions that prohibit you from making choices for positive improvement. Si-ah acts much like the gold-miners pan that swirls away the water of emotion and dirt of falsity exposing the golden nuggets of truth.

Once a thought or feeling has been recognized as not serving or honoring your life, Si-ah transforms its energy. This transformation allows the power of the negative to begin to reinforce what is truth. Once the thought or emotion has no power over you, its energy is absorbed into what is truth.

When Si-ah releases the power of the negative, it retains the pure energy of it within itself acting as a storehouse until the energy is needed. When the physical body becomes endangered by imbalance or disease, Si-ah uses this energy as a warning system and begins to alert the senses. Si-ah is the Essential that stimulates the sensation of something being not quite right. Whether a feeling or a thought, Si-ah increases your awareness of it and starts the activation of the appropriate response.

You may utilize this tool when you can't decide what is wrong or you begin to have a sense of doom and gloom. Focus your awareness on Si-ah's energy during meditation and ask for clarification. When you receive an impression regarding an imbalance, trust yourself and begin to seek necessary techniques to restore balance. Si-ah is one of the Essentials that powers intuition, especially concerning the physical body.

Our emotions often become the major obstacles in acting on our choices. Not wanting to rock the boat or cause discord sometimes is nothing more than a manifestation of fear. We become frozen in fear and subject to the rise and fall of emotional turmoil. When we utilize the power of Si-ah we can break free from overpowering fear and focus more clearly on joy. Emotions assist us in creating excuses for not changing. They are self-perpetuating and gain power over our behavior. Si-ah helps us to recognize the falsity in the word "can't" and know it more truthfully as "won't." With the emotions more focused in joy, we are able to move forward with positive changes and actions. We begin to be more honest with ourselves and recognize where change is needed.

Si-ah also assists us in choosing what words of others hold truth in our life. It is the Essential that helps us release statements not based in fact. Comments that try to convince us we will never make anything of ourselves or are not capable or worthy do not affect us when Si-ah is actively participating in our life. It transforms the falsities and empowers truth enabling us to recognize the wisdom within ourselves to make clear choices.

Affirmations are positive tools in awakening the energy of Si-ah as well as something as simply singing when you are frightened. The joy activated in both of these techniques increases our ability to recognize how unproductive it is to remain in the grasp of fear or doubt.

The essential oil *Citrus Aurantium* moves through your senses to awaken you to Si-ah's existence and clears the obstacles of physical, mental, and emotional toxins that distance you from fully utilizing its energy.

The speed at which Si-ah vibrates is the same as the musical note of D#. Utilizing that tone calls the sense of hearing into experiencing Si-ah's energy and increases the body's ability to recognize its positive potential.

CHAPTER ELEVEN

Ni-mahn

We all find comfort in the familiar. How many times have you looked at a pair of well-worn shoes or a tattered, stained T-shirt that you just don't have the heart to throw out? How often do you wear bright colors or change your hairstyle? Does a snowy day invite you to take a walk or curl up with a book?

Like Jesus did with Lazarus; Ni-mahn calls us to come forth, to move outside our comfort zones and attempt something new.

The first time a skier stands atop a new hillside there is a rush of excitement and anticipation. When a speaker or performer prepares to go on stage they often experience butterflies in their stomach.

What is this feeling? This is where the energy of Ni-mahn resides. When it is activated you may actually feel a physical sensation. It is one of the strongest Essentials in producing a physical sensation. Ni-mahn also works as a warning system that a change of energy is about to occur. That sick feeling in the pit of your stomach or feeling of anticipation is Ni-mahn's way to alert you to change.

Ni-mahn then sets into motion the energy to balance that change.

Many who do not allow the free expression of this Essential find themselves locked into old patterns and prisoners in their own world. In severe cases of obstruction of Ni-mahn people may develop ulcers and become agoraphobic.

For each individual there exists exciting and challenging opportunities in life. Opportunities to expand ourselves to embrace possibilities and grow into joyous relationships and careers. Until we develop and utilize the power stored in this Essential, we hesitate or become fearful and the opportunity passes us by.

As we are growing up we may encounter a teacher or coach that we feel is pushing us too hard by asking us to do things we don't feel we can. If we are unable to draw on the energy of Ni-mahn we become angry and frustrated instead of recognizing that they may see a potential within us that we are not aware of. Ni-mahn feeds you with the ability to try. To attempt to discover if this is an area where you may excel in life and find great joy.

Each person has many inborn or innate talents and it is left to Ni-mahn to assist us in illumining them. Fear of failure or even success is the primary obstacle that we encounter and Ni-mahn has the energy to helps us through that fear.

The need for acceptance within our peer groups suppresses the energy of Ni-mahn. With this energy suppressed we falsely believe that we need to look like, wear the same clothes, talk like, eat, and do all of the same things as our friends.

When Ni-mahn is flowing fully we begin to recognize that these actions truly do not bring us joy and that we are being nothing more than carbon copies of those around us. We find our deeper desires illumined and begin to make choices that will lead us to fulfilling them. We become the trendsetters and find the strength within us to choose for ourselves. We begin to seek out those individuals who walk the path we desire instead of remaining in the place where we began and may even change our circle of friends.

Choosing to become the person that our inner self knows we have the potential to be sometimes requires recreating ourselves. Ni-mahn supplies the necessary energy to make these choices. It allows us to see clearly how we can make a difference in our life and the conditions in the world and drives us to begin. It illumines the choices that will bring us closer to our goals and gives us the determination and energy to make them without hesitation. Ni-mahn allows us to recognize that we have the same right and ability as another and what we perceive, as obstacles are our own fears. The powerful energy of Ni-mahn then moves us beyond those fears and allows us to see clearly when and where change is necessary.

You can begin the process of using this powerful energy by simply replacing words in your vocabulary. Substituting *I will give it my best* for *I can't* begins to refocus the mind to the possibility that you can. Go someplace you have never been. Wear a bright color. Try a new food or drink. Ask someone to lunch. Speak to someone you don't know in an elevator or waiting room. The energy of Ni-mahn will begin to flow and you will find yourself experiencing all kinds of new and exciting opportunities.

The essential oil *Ravensara Aromatica* moves through your senses to awaken you to Ni-mahn's existence and clears the obstacles of physical, mental, and emotional toxins that distance you from fully utilizing its energy.

The speed at which Ni-mahn vibrates is the same as the musical note of E. Utilizing that tone calls the sense of hearing into experiencing Ni-mahn's energy and increases the body's ability to recognize its positive potential.

CHAPTER TWELVE

Bay-larh

When we begin to poll the masses for information we will find that there are as many opinions as there are people willing to give them. The need to check with everyone before making a decision in our own life is an indicator of the blocked flow of the energy of Bay-larh. We do not trust our own instincts. Bay-larh assists us in taking information supplied from others and sorting it out for application in our situations in life.

Bay-larh recognizes that it is not necessary to reinvent the wheel and is able to distinguish which information will carry us more swiftly to our goal. It is important to note that Bay-larh does have a maximum capacity and will tend to only consider the first few sources of information. After that, Bay-larh will become over-stimulated and the information will become a swirling mass of indistinguishable noise. When you bring the energy of Bay-larh into the chaos and confusion of situations, it has the power to lead you to the clarity of positive thought, shutting out words and thoughts that are not in the best interest for you.

Left to our own devices Bay-larh will create for us the ability to recognize our own wisdom and intuition and guide us to choices that best serve our needs without harming another. The compassion and understanding of another's needs and thoughts is enhanced through the energy of this Essential. It awakens within us an awareness of how our choices will affect others. It gently guides us in how to apply our decisions. It gives us a sense of timing and a method of acting on our choices that allows more positive response from the people around us.

Bay-larh contains the wisdom that each of us is given the same ability to become our full potentials. No one is greater or lesser. It allows us to know clearly that we are as deserving and capable as another. Therefore, we do not find ourselves in a constant state of comparison. We do not judge ourselves or others based on choices. We recognize that our soul's desire guides our choices and we learn to allow others to choose as is necessary for them. We come to realize that often when another asks for our opinion they don't really want it. All they may need is justification for the decision they have already made. This awakened ability leads us into more harmonious relationships. It also reveals to us that we may not really be asking for information from another but simply validation of our choices.

The clarity Bay-larh brings into our choices is a more clear path to the expression of our soul. When we can focus on the choice that brings us joy, we become a more joyful being. This joy then spills over in our lives and we find it easier to act on our choices. We become a delight to be with and others will seek out our companionship. We find ourselves surrounded by positive people who reinforce our positive actions. With Bay-larh in balance, the need to complain and cry on everyone's shoulder diminishes. Positive people with exciting things going on in their lives will want to be with us. We will no longer find ourselves continually in crises.

When Bay-larh awakens this ability within us we will also discover the people in our lives who are constantly in crises and recognize the effect that they have on us. How often have you listened repeatedly to someone who never has anything good going on in their life? Everything they try doesn't work and everyone is against them. Nothing ever changes. Every suggestion or ideas for positive change has a million excuses for why it won't work for them. You're stronger. You're smarter. It might work for you but they don't have your abilities. How do you feel after a long telephone call from them? Exhausted, frustrated, heavy, depressed? Bay-larh's energy helps you identify these situations and people. It empowers you with the ability to begin to utilize your time and energy more wisely. It provides you with the wisdom necessary to eliminate these situations and people from your life in a manner that does not harm you or them.

Complimenting another, putting a quarter in someone's expired parking meter, withholding your opinion when not asked, are all random acts of kindness that assist in awakening the energy of Bay-larh.

The essential oil *Anethum Graveolens* moves through your senses to awaken you to Bay-larh's existence and clears the obstacles of physical, mental, and emotional toxins that distance you from fully utilizing its energy.

The speed at which Bay-larh vibrates is the same as the musical note of F. Utilizing that tone calls the sense of hearing into experiencing Bay-larh's energy and increases the body's ability to recognize its positive potential.

CHAPTER THIRTEEN

Hol-mahn

Whether female or male we all have the ability to love and nurture ourselves and others. We all have the capability of feeling joy at the success of ourselves and others. We all can celebrate when a baby takes a first step or says a first word. This is the aspect of all of us that is defined as the Goddess energy because of its mothering instincts. Whether female or male, we all contain it. It does not make us vulnerable or weak. In fact, it makes us stronger. It requires a strong person to pursue growth and forgive clouded judgment that leads to inappropriate choices. Hol-mahn is that source of strength. Through that strength, we look at the world the same as we would our own child. We access the ability to lovingly protect that child from harm. We discover how to utilize our thoughts, words, and deeds to challenge acts of anger, hatred, or bigotry in nonviolent ways.

With the energy of Hol-mahn integrated into our lives we can discover our true passion. Once discovered, Hol-mahn will provide the drive to accomplish our dreams and expand them beyond our thinking. It will reveal to us where our most powerful potential lies and gently guide us toward choices and actions that bring about the most positive growth.

Hol-mahn will integrate into our thinking a true knowing of our own strengths and begin to offer us encouragement in our wise choices. Once capable of recognizing this we are able to give and do our best strictly for the sense of satisfaction and joy we feel when we do. Our choices empowered by Hol-mahn will be based in the peace and love we receive from within and not the reactions and words of others.

The force of Hol-mahn is the power of love. Love that is eternal and recognizes each individual as worthy of joy and happiness. This love does not demand acceptance and recognizes when its expression is unwanted. The love contained within Hol-mahn is comparable to that of a mother's love for her child. Hol-mahn's love always finds the best qualities within an individual and encourages those choices that express them.

When fully integrated, Hol-mahn's energy directs our life in paths of fulfillment. It helps us to learn how to love without requirement. Too often we hear the words "if you love me you would." Hol-mahn shows us that true love has no expectation of behavior or even return. We begin to love for the sake of loving, not for the sake of gratification. When we do so our whole being begins to fill with the power of Hol-mahn and the same type of love is attracted to us.

With this Essential operating effectively we begin to make choices that leads us to people who can love and accept us as we are because we have learned to love and accept ourselves. Our decisions will direct us to people and places that love us as powerfully as we love ourselves. The reverse is as powerfully true. For as we love, so shall we be loved. Hol-mahn shows us that love is the ability to accept the good and potential within ourselves. If we block the flow of this Essential we find ourselves in relationships that are demanding and abusive. We arrive there because we make choices without Hol-mahn's integration and begin to believe that these types of relationships are all that we are worthy of. We put ourselves in places with people who believe the same and our choices keep us there.

Sending a card without an occasion or calling just to say hello helps you to become more integrated into the power of Hol-mahn. Buying yourself something nice or taking yourself out to dinner someplace special allows Hol-mahn to begin positive expression in your life.

The essential oil *Nardostachys Jatamansi* moves through your senses to awaken you to Hol-mahn's existence and clears the obstacles of physical, mental, and emotional toxins that distance you from fully utilizing its energy.

The speed at which Hol-mahn vibrates is the same as the musical note of F#.

Utilizing that tone calls the sense of hearing into experiencing Hol-mahn's energy and increases the body's ability to recognize its positive potential.

CHAPTER FOURTEEN
Tol-mahr

Have you ever asked, "How many times do I have to tell you?" Have you ever been asked, "Did you hear me? Don't you remember me telling you? Why didn't you tell me?" How many times have you wished you hadn't said something and that you could take it back? Words are a powerful energy that once set in motion can never be destroyed. Their power can be dissipated but it will always remain.

In our physical existence, there is nothing more powerful than words. They can end relationships, friendships, begin wars, destroy confidence, and change lives forever. They can also create lasting relationships, friendships, end wars, build self esteem, and positively change lives. When the Essential Tol-mahr is operating clearly, it awakens our ability to wisely and effectively choose our words.

According to Biblical accounts our entire existence began with words when God said Tol-mahr accesses that original creative power and gives us the wisdom to choose words that create what we desire in this life experience. This wisdom comes from that Divine will to create joy and positive experiences in our life and Tol-mahr is our key to unlock that potential. It allows us to recognize when we have lost focus of the will of all creation and have begun to utilize our potential for the temporary pleasures. Things that our mind would have us believe are real.

Tol-mahr shows us the long-term effect of our choice of words and empowers us to think before we speak. It reveals to us when we are attempting to manipulate others and creates the awareness of the responsibility that it brings. If we choose words that are meant to intentionally hurt another then we are responsible for the pain it creates in their life.

Tol-mahr also is capable of eliminating the fear that prohibits us from speaking forth when we recognize injustice in our life. When we find ourselves in relationships or careers that become detrimental to our physical, emotional, or mental health, Tol-mahr drives us to speak up. It creates the use of words that will bring about the change of the situations to positive ones. Tol-mahr teaches us that words spoken in anger create angry responses and converts anger into positive action. It removes fear from our words so that fear does not grow and entrap us where we are not happy and healthy. It introduces us to Divine timing and allows us to see clearly where our words will most effectively bring about desired change.

Within our being dwells the remembrance of all things good and with Tol-mahr active, we are awakened as to how to bring them into being. This remembrance is the accumulation of our joyful experiences and how they came into being. Tol-mahr allows us to recognize how all of creation supplements our life experience through its creation of joy without our conscious participation. The beauty of a sunset. The rainbow in a storm. The hush of a falling snow. The morning song of a bird. A small animal curling up to its mother. The clean smell after a spring rain. Tol-mahr recognizes the positive effect of all of these things and calls us to take a moment to bring the joy of their existence into our life. Joy is increased when we choose to participate in it and Tol-mahr offers us that ability.

With Tol-mahr in balance we can see what really matters in our life. We then are able to effectively use our energy in areas that will create what we seek. No longer will we waste our words but will begin to use them to make choices that build a more healthy and happy life. We will recognize when to speak and when to remain silent. We will acquire the wisdom that sometimes the most powerful words are those that go unspoken.

Simple acts like refusing to engage in gossip or join in running someone down are powerful beginnings toward aligning with Tol-mahr's energy. Acts such as these may even offer another the opportunity to choose the same and begin to bring them into balance. Try taking I told you so out of your vocabulary. Take just one day and choose not to watch, read, or listen to negative news or words. See how different your day goes.

The essential oil *Mentha Spicata* moves through your senses to awaken you to Tol-mahr's existence and clears the obstacles of physical, mental, and emotional toxins that distance you from fully utilizing its energy.

The speed at which Tol-mahr vibrates is the same as the musical note of G. Utilizing that tone calls the sense of hearing into experiencing Tol-mahr's energy and increases the body's ability to recognize its positive potential.

CHAPTER FIFTEEN

Cal-mahr

So many precious moments and joyful loving experiences are missed because we are caught up in the noise and confusion of the world. Our minds become so polluted with untrue and unfounded fears and doubts that we can no longer see the potential of our dreams. We allow ourselves to see only how our lives are difficult. We cannot open ourselves to the inspiration for ways to initiate change.

Within the energy of Cal-mahr there lies the illumination that we do not walk this earth alone. Cal-mahr holds the key to opening ourselves to the flow of Divine inspiration and teaches us how to make choices that will create new and exciting opportunities.

When standing on a mountaintop we are given the opportunity to see the world from a clearer perspective. We begin to see how the patterns of the earth blend together to form a beautiful tapestry of life and living. We understand how creation is not random, and our existence is an integral part of a much larger picture. A snapshot in time. A design that will reveal itself to us when we allow Cal-mahr to shine forth on it.

While standing in this awareness we are offered clarity of choice and the wisdom to see how they weave into the fabric of our being. Cal-mahr parts the clouds of our limited thinking and shines like the sun of a new day. It illumines the dark areas of our life and brings light into our awareness enabling us to choose joy, choose light, and choose love.

Those positive thoughts that just pop into our head are able to do so when Cal-mahr is operating fully. The inspiration to do something in a certain way, say something at a certain time and change the way we look at our experiences is powered by Cal-mahr. It allows us to more fully utilize the wisdom of Divine Law to perpetuate change.

Cal-mahr accesses the truth that what we set into motion in our lives and upon the face of the earth does indeed return to us. It gives us understanding of how our life is an accumulation of experiences and shows us the positive effects they have to offer. It calls us to renew the connectedness of our thoughts with our physical well being and the ability to create an avenue for the expression of our spirit.

When we are at peace with our actions and surroundings, choices become easy. When we are healthy, happy, and prosperous the world is a more inviting place. We can choose more quickly and appropriately and do not spend long hours in confusion and doubt. This can be created for us when we access the energy of Cal-mahr and act upon the inspirations that gently guide us toward our goals.

Keeping a journal of your dreams and thoughts allows you to begin to see the paths you are being inspired to take. This brings to your conscious awareness areas of your life that are not fully being expressed.

The essential oil *Commiphora Myrrha* moves through your senses to awaken you to Cal-mahr's existence and clears the obstacles of physical, mental, and emotional toxins that distance you from fully utilizing its energy.

The speed at which Cal-mahr vibrates is the same as the musical note of G#. Utilizing that tone calls the sense of hearing into experiencing Cal-mahr's energy and increases the body's ability to recognize its positive potential.

CHAPTER SIXTEEN

Vi-mahn

When you feel like your choice is leading you away from your goal, Vi-mahn is attempting to keep you focused on what you truly desire. This Essential contains the clarity of your actions and choices; how they integrate into your life. It is the gentle nudge that keeps you away from the should have, could have, and if onlys. It guides you in the choice of action that will clear the obstacles from your path.

We have great tendencies to make our lives more difficult than they need to be. Left to the guidance of our mental minds and emotions we continually create challenges in order to satisfy a sense of accomplishment. If we utilize the abilities of Vi-mahn, challenges become less frequent and opportunities to succeed become prevalent.

We can begin to recognize that some of our behaviors are the things about others that irritate us the most. Empowered with this wisdom through Vi-mahn we can then enter into necessary change. We stop trying to fix others and refocus on where we need to choose differently. We are not as concerned with what we perceive as others mistakes but do become aware of how choices affect them.

Vi-mahn helps us to see, often through the actions of others, how every action affects the whole. We begin to recognize that indeed the whole is the sum of its parts. When we lose sight of how we fit into the greater scheme of life, Vi-mahn allows us to see how our choices produce reactions from others. If something keeps telling us that we need to help someone and we choose differently, we may discover later that they injured themselves by attempting it alone.

Vi-mahn integrates into our actions the ability to act clearly and with purpose when opportunities present themselves. It guides us to people, places, and choices that will encourage our dreams to flourish. It is the soil that feeds the flowering of our soul.

As water seeks its own level so Vi-mahn brings us to a point of balance within our life experiences. It teaches us to recognize how each step brings us closer to making our dreams a reality and how all rivers do flow to the sea. Armed with this awareness we are able to find the real purpose in our actions and maintain forward movement.

Vi-mahn leads us to discover how each event in our life serves our progression. Whether we learn how to achieve or how not to achieve each experience teaches us something. Vi-mahn integrates that wisdom and brings it back into our awareness when we face similar situations. It gives us the power to choose differently this time. It enables us to make educated decisions and avoid the pitfalls of the past. Vi-mahn takes experience and turns it into wisdom that will best serve us.

Practice following that feeling in choices. Allow yourself to begin with little things that are not so intimidating to begin to trust your intuition. Try to guess who is on the phone when it rings. When you build up your confidence, try answering it using their name. If you feel like you need to take a different route home from work, do it and listen to the radio or check the next day's paper for construction or delays on your normal route.

The essential oil *Jasminum Officianle* moves through your senses to awaken you to Vi-mahn's existence and clears the obstacles of physical, mental, and emotional toxins that distance you from fully utilizing its energy.

The speed at which Vi-mahn vibrates is the same as the musical note of A. Utilizing that tone calls the sense of hearing into experiencing Vi-mahn's energy and increases the body's ability to recognize its positive potential.

CHAPTER SEVENTEEN

Hal-rai

When we allow other's thoughts and events in their lives to consume us we turn over control of our own life to them. We begin to think that they know us better than we know ourselves. We wait for them to tell us what we are good at and how we should achieve. We hesitate to move forward until we know that someone else approves of the direction.

The energy of Hal-rai demands that we recognize responsibility for our life. It powerfully illumines the choices that will keep things simple. The energy of this Essential is like the water rides at an amusement park. You climb into a log that rides upon water in a channel. It carries you in the direction to reach your goal. The channel keeps you on track and leads you to the completion of the ride. Hal-rai requests that you claim your ticket by realizing that the ride was created for your enjoyment. Without your participation it has no purpose. Once you are willing to climb on board, the energy of Hal-rai will direct the flow in ways that remain balanced and keep you upright. The clear flow of Hal-rai's energy doesn't mean you won't get wet occasionally, but at least you will be able to laugh at yourself.

The biggest obstacle you will encounter as Hal-rai begins to carry you swiftly toward the realization of your dreams is the illusion that you no longer need the channel. The ego begins to bask in the effects of your prosperity, continued health, and happiness and attempts to convince you that the world owes you nothing less. When this occurs Hal-rai will offer you a situation to help you realize that God is the source of wisdom that guides you in your most productive choices. Hal-rai is the bridge that enables you to touch into that wisdom. The ego can be a powerful force in your life. It constantly renews the desire of your spirit to do and be no less than your best. When the ego looses it focus it can break the vital connection to Hal-rai. It then attempts to control the direction of your path at any cost. Hal-rai becomes clouded and the accolades of the world become more important than fulfillment of your potential. Hal-rai refocuses you to recognize, "What have you gained if you conquer the world but lose your soul?"

Once the ego is brought into harmony with the energy of Hal-rai, it can drive you to accomplish great things. Hal-rai is the compass of your ship and your spirit is its captain. With these two elements working in harmony, you may not conquer the world but opportunities to experience it in the greatest joy will be provided.

The next time you work on a project that requires someone's assistance, put them in the forefront for praise. Send an anonymous flower arrangement to someone. These are ways you can begin to align yourself with the available power of Hal-rai and bring it more actively into your life.

The essential oil *Larus Nobilis* moves through your senses to awaken you to Hal-rai's existence and clears the obstacles of physical, mental, and emotional toxins that distance you from fully utilizing its energy.

The speed at which Hal-rai vibrates is the same as the musical note of B flat. Utilizing that tone calls the sense of hearing into experiencing Hal-rai's energy and increases the body's ability to recognize its positive potential.

CHAPTER EIGHTEEN

Hal-mard

There are many times in all of our lives when we don't know where we can find the strength to continue. We see things in our life in need of change. It seems like the ability to make those changes is more than we have. We feel alone and the burden of life has becomes too heavy.

Hal-mard is the light that shines through that darkness. It illumines the joy and happiness that awaits us in the next step. Hal-mard clears our vision and allows us to see the positive potential that each moment holds. When this Essential is blended into our life, it makes lemonade out of what we thought was bitter fruit.

Hal-mard is the lighthouse on the shore that allows us to clearly see dangerous choices, even in the midst of our turmoil. It allows us to recognize the boulders and guides us in clear channels of opportunities. When we become too focused on whether this person thinks we are smart, or that person thinks we are cute, Hal-mard shows us how this misspent energy depletes us for things that truly matter.

Hal-mard reminds us that we are all equal when stripped of the coverings of race and gender. It reminds us that there is only one race; The human race. It also helps us to recognize how all of creation is available to enhance our choices toward positive change. It brings an awareness of the importance of each of these aspects. It lets us recognize how all choices are intertwined.

If you are hungry and stop in your local market, you anticipate that everything you need will be there to sustain you. You don't consider all of the choices necessary to provide you with what you desire. What if farmers had felt it was too much work to plant the crops to feed you and the livestock? What if no one was willing to work at a low wage as a laborer to cultivate the harvest and load the trucks? What if the drivers weren't in the mood to deal with traffic? What if the store owner forgot to pay the rent and the doors were locked? These are just a few of the choices that must be made in order for you to walk into the market, make your purchase, and be fed.

Hal-mard shows us the power of our choices and how each one affects the whole. It guides us to those choices and inspires us to continually choose in ways that will most greatly increase our life, and thereby the lives of those around us.

Start incorporating Hal-mard's energy into your life by doing such simple things as leaving a bigger tip and thanking your server. When you become more aware of Hal-mard's power try getting someone to understand who you are talking about without using their race in your description. When they ask why you didn't mention their race, tell them that you didn't notice or feel that it was their most outstanding quality. See if you can not notice race. Do something that inspires you.

The essential oil Hyssop moves through your senses to awaken you to Hal-mard's existence and clears the obstacles of physical, mental, and emotional toxins that distance you from fully utilizing its energy.

The speed at which Hal-mard vibrates is the same as the musical note of B. Utilizing that tone calls the sense of hearing into experiencing Hal-mard's energy and increases the body's ability to recognize its positive potential.

CHAPTER NINETEEN
Hal-lái

Within the heart of all creation there is a pulse that continues to beat in rhythm, harmony, and balance. Hal-lái integrates into your being the awareness of its source and teaches you to keep in step. It opens you to the memory that there is nothing new upon the earth, that all things have been, are now, and will continue to be.

Hal-lái is The Christmas Carol of our own life. It shows how what you do in this moment forever changes the future. It is the ultimate source for the aligning with the energy to create change. Hal-lái recognizes you as an active part in the wholeness of all that is. If you will allow it, Hal-lái guides you to remember. Remember that you are love and you are loved. No matter where you may journey, or what you may experience there is always a loving heart and open arms waiting to receive you.

Hal-lái is the threshold you must come to in order to begin to fully understand why life exists and why you are in it. It is the gentle master that lifts up the tired and worn violin and brings forth beautiful music. Hal-lái teaches you how to create the same harmony in all of your actions so that the full symphony may be experienced.

The wisdom that is accessible through the energy of Hal-lái gives you the tools needed in life. It focuses on the big T Truths. It reveals the ever-changing truths that the world would offer. It then guides you to utilize the power of these Truths to bring about your ultimate health, joy, prosperity, and potential.

The most powerful tool you can use to integrate the power of Hal-lái into your life is prayer. Create a running dialogue with the heart of God directly from your heart. Talk to that heart as you would a best friend anytime, anywhere. It doesn't require words and it doesn't require a specific format. The heart of God already knows how you feel but is always willing to listen.

The essential oil Angelica moves through your senses to awaken you to Hal-lái's existence and clears the obstacles of physical, mental, and emotional toxins that distance you from fully utilizing its energy.

The speed at which Hal-lái vibrates is the same as the musical note of C above middle C. Utilizing that tone calls the sense of hearing into experiencing Hal-lái's energy and increases the body's ability to recognize its positive potential.

CHAPTER TWENTY

The Essentials of Being

How do we initiate change within ourselves? How do we then align with the ability to awaken oneness with the indwelling spirit? How do we bring ourselves into full illumination?

You must first have understanding to begin to utilize the power of change and illumination of spirit. Here you are offered 12 Essentials of being. The information for each Essential is presented in three parts: The Energy Center, The Physical Body System with Indicators of Imbalance, and The spiritual Precept.

The Energy Center is often referred to as a chakra. In this section you will find a quick reference for: the Primary Active Energy, the Musical Note, the Balancing Color, the Primary Balancing Essential Oil, the Location, Other Names, and Balanced Characteristics associated with the essential. The centers are addressed utilizing their Atlantian designation. Using the color, essential oil and sounding the Atlantian designation in its musical note, further enhances awakening the soul's remembrance. The more physical senses you utilize, the swifter your progress. This awakening begins the process that integrates your potential into the illumination of your being.

The Physical System is the body system of the Essential being brought into balance in your process of integration and illumination. A system is a collection of organs and structures sharing a common function. Organs and structures of a single system occupy diverse regions in the body and are not necessarily grouped together. Due to the diversified functions of the Central Nervous System and the Peripheral Nervous System they have been presented individually. The Lymphatic System is integral to the Immune System, therefore they have been combined.

The Indicators of Imbalance for each Essential is given so you may recognize your body's early warning system. When you begin to notice difficulties with the associated areas of the body you are asked to examine all aspects of the Essential for possible areas in need of attention.

Not all disease is solely a product of an Essential being out of balance. You will find though, that as the Essential is brought back into balance, the healing of the body will be greatly enhanced. To encourage the full healing you should always seek the assistance of your health care provider whether you choose natural/alternative or traditional medical treatment. We believe in integrated medicine and encourage you to use the information presented here in conjunction with active treatment, to bring the whole of your being back into participation in your healing process. We are not medical doctors and do not presume to diagnose or prescribe. This information is not to be construed as a substitute for medical treatment. It is presented as a possible supplement. You should always consult with your health care provider before beginning any protocol.

Be aware of what you are doing. It is essential that you actively participate in your healing process and become aware of what you are doing. Whatever supplements you choose, become educated on their effects and uses. If your child came to you with a hand full of drugs someone gave them, would you allow them to take them? Know what you are putting into your body, whether it is synthetic or natural. Not all natural products are safe in combination with other products. Carbon monoxide and crude oil are natural, but would you want to eat or drink them?

Some individuals may bring limitation and disease into their life due to unfinished learning experiences of past lives. Other individuals may choose to manifest limitation or disease in order to serve the growth of those around them. The individuals who make this choice are great gifts in our lives and true masters of unconditional love.

A Precept is defined as a spiritual, general rule of action guiding your soul. They are spiritual guidance for physical action, much like parables. The precept becomes action, when you incorporate its principles into your thoughts, words and deeds.

The Essentials are given in an order, but as you begin to bring them into balance, you will find yourself vacillating from one to the other. Each Essential builds upon the other but they also move within each other.

The knowledge of the information of the Essentials is incomplete without your action. When offered here the information exists only as a profession of love. It is only a vibration, a concept in motion. It is only energy. Without the activation of these essentials within you, these words are but infertile seeds upon barren ground. Their purpose lies within your being. They can serve no one if they cannot be internalized and become balanced.

As you begin to work with each one individually, you begin to blend those aspects and qualities into the illumination and activation of your spirit. This blending awakens your innate healing ability and prepares you to fully utilize your potential. You are encouraged to work with each Essential separately to incorporate its balance. As you immerse yourself fully into each Essential you begin the process of blending all twelve into balance. Once you have achieved balance within one area, move to the next. The goals are: to awaken your innate healing ability and divine wisdom, integrate the potential and power of your spirit, and illumine the whole of your being into a life of love and joy.

When you achieve balance within an Essential, you find the Physical System it addresses, the principles of the energy, and the precept begin to work in harmony. With this harmony established, your life becomes filled with joy and prosperity. Your choices are guided gently along your path to personal power.

Just as Mother Teresa, we must speak fewer words and become God in action. We must set aside our fear of the untouchables and reach out through the darkness. So let us begin and may we be guided upon this path.

Hal-lái 12
11 Hal-mard
Hal-rai 10
9 Vi-mahn
Cal-mahr 8
7 Tol-mahr
Hol-mahn 6
5 Bay-lahr
Ni-mahn 4
3 Si-ah
Re-ah 2

1 Ei-ahn

How to calculate your personal centers:

Write down your birthdate like this:

Month
Day
+Year

Add up each column.

11
3
+1958
1972

Then add up the row of numbers that you get.

1+9+7+2 = 19

If the number is less than 12 you are done. If it is more, add those two numbers together again.

1+9= 10

Count from the 1st Energy Center (Ei-ahn) up until you have reached your number.

This is your **physical** center. The 10th Center up on the chart is Hal-rai.

Count from your physical center up and back around (starting at the bottom, Ei-ahn) until you have reached your number.

This is your **spiritual** center. Ten more centers up and around is Cal-mahr.

Therefore, if you were born on 11/3/58 you are a Hal-rai/ Cal-mahr.

EI-AHN

ENERGY SYSTEM

PRIMARY ACTIVE ENERGY: Integration

RESONATES TO THE MUSICAL NOTE: C#

BALANCING COLOR: Brown

PRIMARY BALANCING ESSENTIAL OIL: *Abies Alba*

LOCATION: 6 inches below the earth centered between the feet

OTHER NAMES: Earth Star

BALANCED CHARACTERISTICS:

- Anchors your spirit to earth
- Renews personal balance and harmony
- Integrates our true self into the physical body
- Allows us to recognize the beauty of all creation
- Helps us to nurture others and ourselves
- Allows us to actively participate in returning the earth to balance
- Draws the power of your spirit through the body
- Creates a reverence for and harmony with nature
- Renews the strength of spiritual understanding and truth
- Establishes the power of re-creating your reality

Body System

SKELETAL SYSTEM: The skeletal system is the jointed framework of rigid bones that supports the soft tissues of the body. There are 206 bones in the adult skeletal system. As a system, the bones give the body its shape; they form cages and boxes that protect fragile organs; and they form a complicated lever system that assists in body movements.

There are two main parts of the skeletal system: the axial skeleton and the appendicular skeleton. The axial skeleton consists of the skull, the spine, and the rib cage. All of these axial bones provide protection for vital parts of the body.

The appendicular skeleton consists of the shoulder and hip girdles and the arm and leg bones. The pelvic or hip girdle protects the internal organs of the reproductive and urinary systems; but the main function is movement.

At the joints, the ends of the bones are shaped to fit into each other. Some movable joints can move freely in any direction, such as the joints at the shoulder and the hip. Other joints, such as the knee and elbow joints, can move in only one direction.

Indicators of Imbalance

Just as the skeletal system permits movement of the body, when Ei-ahn is in balance we move easily from one experience to another. We are capable of seeing all options and moving in the appropriate choices. When Ei-ahn is out of balance we become rigid in our opinions, unable to see or consider alternatives. Our physical body often responds with arthritis and painful joints.

The skeletal system also supports and protects the body and enables us to stand erect. When Ei-ahn is out of balance we have difficulties standing strong in our decisions and protecting ourselves from the influence of others. We have a tendency to withdraw from the pressures of everyday life and may enter into varying degrees of depression.

PRECEPT

The precept that you will address with Ei-ahn is that of blending of your physical reality with your spiritual being; learning how those two blend in harmony. It is an awareness of your physical body and how it appears, in balance or imbalance. It is an awareness of how you interact with your physical surroundings and utilize your spiritual beliefs. You must be in harmony with the earth and your physical reality to be able to synthesize your spiritual beliefs. This brings about harmony and blending.

If you learn to become one with physical awareness you are facilitating your opportunity to blend it into a spiritual awareness. To manifest the ability to blend what are too often two separate worlds you must spend regular time in meditation. Meditation will give you direction and clarity. Your heart must be open to the spiritual aspect of your being in order to effect change upon your physical world.

Meditation is a blending of physical and spiritual awareness. For in your physical existence you are aware of your need for spiritual interaction. It is imperative in slowing down your physical activity so that your spirit has time to grow. Meditation is an essential part of all precepts. How can you center energy and learn to work with it when you do not practice?

If your physical being is not familiar with energy flows, it becomes difficult for you to allow that flow, or to activate it within you. Meditation is a very appropriate time to become aware of energies and begin to blend them into your physical life. It is no more appropriate though to attempt to walk only in the spirit than it is to focus only in the physical. If you walk around constantly in spiritual awareness you are denying the physical existence. Even in the worst circumstances of a physical reality there can be a spiritual expression.

Sometimes you seek a physical experience and do not realize when that has been given to you. When you seek in prayer you always have time to ask, demand and beg but seldom do you have time to recognize the response. This lack of recognition exists because you have not learned to blend physical and spiritual needs. Many times we pray for a desire in the physical world and fail to recognize the response from spirit. If you are praying and affirming for someone in your life to love you unconditionally, you may not realize that spirit has responded. Your answer may be a pet that allows you to be who you are, and loves you anyway.

Sometimes you more quickly receive what you desire when you quit asking for it. You are so busy trying to direct spirit in a physical manifestation of your desires you miss it when it comes. Often you do recognize it, because it is not exactly what you meant. It may be what you asked for but it is not exactly what you meant.

The energy of your desire, or spirit of it, has no physical limitation but your perception of its physical manifestation limits its ability to be.

RE-AH

PRIMARY ACTIVE ENERGY: Awakening

RESONATES TO THE MUSICAL NOTE: D

BALANCING COLOR: Red

PRIMARY BALANCING ESSENTIAL OIL: *Pelargonium Graveolens*

LOCATION: Tip of the tailbone at the reproductive organs

OTHER NAMES: Root chakra

BALANCED CHARACTERISTICS:

- Stimulates personal power
- Renews creative energy
- Allows us to recognize what brings us joy or anger to our lives
- Releases the hold of fears ingrained by beliefs of parents and past experience
- Brings an awareness of the light and joy of an earthly experience and overcomes the illusion of death
- Blends the power of unconditional love into action toward personal growth and positive change
- Transmutes fear-based reactions to life into powerful steps to awaken individuality
- Empowers enlightened behavior over the response of the masses

REPRODUCTIVE SYSTEM: The reproductive system in the male consists of the penis, the testes, the scrotum, a series of ducts, and a number of glands. The male sex hormone stimulates the development of ducts and glands of the reproductive system generally between 11 and 14 years of age as well as secondary sex characteristics.

The primary organ of the female reproductive system is the ovary, which produces the ova and secretes the hormones estrogen and progesterone. The uterus serves as a site for implantation and nourishment of the embryo. The vagina receives the semen from the penis and transmits it to the uterus and acts as a birth canal from the uterus to the outside for the newborn.

The breast, in both male and female is an area of fatty fibrous tissue, with associated nerves and blood and lymphatic vessels. Packed within the tissue is a collection of branching ducts. In the male and non-pregnant female, these ducts are undeveloped. The lymphatic vessels are an important part of the breast: they drain the fat portion of the milk produced during nursing. They also transfer infected material or cancer cells from the breast to more distant parts.

INDICATORS OF IMBALANCE

When Re-ah is out of balance we find ourselves immobilized in old thinking; unable to utilize our inner strength to implement creative possibilities. We remain in the limitations of our ancestors, too fearful to break the patterns of their thinking and initiate original thought. Imbalances of Re-ah may manifest in difficulties with: fertility, sexual performance, fibrous tissue in the breast, and prostate enlargement. In severe cases these conditions may progress into malignancy.

This is the energy where most people dwell. They live within their fears. There is a great need to abolish your fears, to put them aside. Often people think, "What will it take for me to overcome these fears?" Many people have many fears of different things. A fear of change. A fear of lack.

If you have a fear of lack, of not having physical things, then all of your focus and intent is placed within that fear. The fear of not having the car you want, the home you want, having nothing in your life. What would it take to abolish this fear, to be rid of it? Some might think $5000.00 would get rid of my fear. But would it really? You may be concerned about where you are going to get that amount, how you are going to distribute it, will you have to pay it back. Would it resolve everything or would it be a temporary fix?

You need then to look at what it would take to completely abolish that fear. Perhaps you could begin by using an affirmation to absolve the fear. To set your self free from the fear and guilt.

Forgive yourself for allowing a fear to control and direct your life. Forgive yourself for allowing fear to control your actions, your words, your goals. When you allow fears to exist you give them your inner power. By giving your fears your power, you have increased their power. You have lost the focus that if love directs you then fear cannot exist. "There is no fear in love, but perfect love casts out fear. For fear has to do with punishment, and he who fears is not perfected in love." (I John 4:18)

A suggested affirmation to begin to work with the ability to take back your control and release fear is: "I absolve, I release, I forgive all obstacles that stand between my potential and me. I now open my heart to receive."

Words are not necessary but they are a tool that you can utilize to assist you in directing your energy. Any affirmation that you utilize is best spoken three times.

Then your body, your mind and your spirit can come into agreement with what you are saying.

Fear is not only those things that frighten you. There are many energies of fear and sometimes you do not recognize all of them. Sometimes you do not understand that they are fears. For example; judgments are fears, measurements are fears. Of course you can recognize the feeling of lack as a fear as well as the fear of snakes or spiders. These things are apparent fears.

When you begin to do something and do not give it all of the energy you are capable of, it is because of fear. You may feel that you are not giving it all of your available energy because you don't want to or you're not in the mood, but often times it is truly an expression of fear. This fear is the hesitancy to give because of the unknown response. Many of these types of hidden fears lie in the fear of failure. These fears set into motion the ability to sabotage yourself, to prove to yourself what you fear is true.

Then you give your fear strength. If you don't know if you can do something but you are going to try, there is still a part of your being that does not believe that you can succeed. There is a part of your being that does not believe in yourself. Then you set into motion the energy to enable the fear to be truth.

If you are ready to attempt to release your fears you must first recognize them. It does not mean that you have to literally face them, but it does mean that you have to become aware of them. When you begin to address your fears as a part of you, you may begin to work with no longer allowing them to control you. This allows your spirit freedom. Freedom from fear, freedom from lack, freedom from want, freedom from the unknown and things you do not understand. You will be allowing your spirit to begin the experience of light and love.

Working with this energy does not mean you have to combat your fears, battle with them or overcome them. If you are trying to overcome them then you are giving them power. You are saying that they are something that has more power than you. When you are trying to work with something and you are working against its will, and with your will, you are trying to overcome it. Think more of coming into harmony with it and then utilizing its energy.

The more you fight with something the more it resists. In battles you become frustrated and angry which, in turn, makes your energy in the same as what you battle. You loose focus of your path when you allow anger to become so large that you no longer control it. You have given your abilities to the anger and frustration. When you can learn to direct the energies of your fears, you can utilize the same energy to build instead of destroy.

You must allow that energy to flow, for it is real within you but you can redirect its path. Whether in fear and anxiety you begin to read a book that relaxes you or in a feeling of loneliness you call someone, you are utilizing the energy of the fear to create its resolution.

When working with this precept, you cannot try to judge if you have accomplished it as well or better than someone else. For in that measurement you are again establishing a fear in your own heart that you are not as capable. If you are afraid of snakes it does not mean that, through the power of this precept, you suddenly are no longer fearful of them. It does mean that you do not allow that fear to prevent you from taking a walk in the woods to enjoy nature. You do not allow that fear to prevent you from continuing in life. You do not give it control over your thoughts and actions. When you take back control of your life from fear, at some point in your life you will find that the fear no longer exists. You may not even know when or how it disappeared.

Fear is the power of the darkness. It shadows your ability to awaken the power of love, or light, within you. Fear takes control of your actions and separates you from success.

SI-AH

ENERGY SYSTEM

PRIMARY ACTIVE ENERGY: Awakening

RESONATES TO THE MUSICAL NOTE: D#

BALANCING COLOR: Yellow

PRIMARY BALANCING ESSENTIAL OIL: *Citrus Aurantium*

LOCATION: Between the reproductive organs and navel, two to three inches to the left

OTHER NAMES: Spleen chakra

BALANCED CHARACTERISTICS:

- Filters negative thoughts and evaluates them for validity in your life
- Renews mental clarity and wisdom
- Storehouse of abundant energy
- Clears residue of thoughts and emotions that no longer honor us
- Releases fears
- Stimulates regeneration of the physical body
- Assists in revealing the source of physical imbalance
- Eliminates the control of the emotions over our choices
- Allows choices to be made in clear thought

URINARY SYSTEM: The urinary system's primary concern is the conservation of water and maintaining a neutral acid-based balance in the fluids of the body. The system consists of two kidneys where blood is filtered and excess water and waste products are released as urine, two urethras the tubes from the kidneys to the bladder, the bladder where urine is stored, and the urethra, the tube that leads from the bladder to the outside of the body.

About 1300ml of blood flows through both kidneys per minute. Less than 0.7ml is then excreted as urine. The kidneys are truly masters of water conservation.

The urinary system is a pathway for elimination of nonessential by-products and toxins that are all dissolved in a small amount of water. What is excreted as waste in one second may be retained in the next.

Two different kinds of imbalance may affect the urinary tract: infection or obstruction. Either of these may damage the kidneys if not brought back into balance. Obstruction can occur because of kidney stones or, in the male, and enlarged prostate. Infections may begin at the opening to the outside of the body and move upward.

Indicators of Imbalance

The urinary system filters and eliminates toxins and those things that no longer serve or honor the body renewing clarity of the body fluids. Si-ah filters negative thinking so that we may regain mental clarity and awaken wisdom. When Si-ah is out of balance we find ourselves focused on negative thoughts and fears obstructed from moving forward wisely. These imbalances may reflect in the physical body in the form of frequent bladder infections and/or kidney stones. When we allow that which no longer serves or honors us to continue to remain in our thinking it grows in power infecting our every action. It forces us to choose based on outside influences.

We will empower harmony and balance within our own lives and cease to empower disease and imbalance. We believe that at some point in our lives, disease will strike and we will die. When we extend this belief to give power to that disease, it then becomes a self-fulfilling prophecy. We often create disease to stop hurting mentally and emotionally and to find peace and joy. The creation of this disease is not because of our inability to find these things but often because we are too tired to try. We feel that we are incapable of living in full peace and joy in a physical existence. Therefore, we allow imbalance within our physical being. This proves its imperfection. If that part of our understanding which allows disease within us, or creates ways for it to manifest directs our will, then we will utilize that disease as our way out.

But, in our own fears, we create ways to prevent that death, just in case. We discover medicines, therapies and all forms of remedies to adjust the manifestations of our fear. We don't see these imbalances and diseases as creations of our fears and error thinking. We spend our lives trying to understand the cause and find the solution instead of seeking truth. If we see the aspect of that love in the practice of medicine, technology, herbs, touch or faith healing then each of these will serve us well. But until we are willing to look at what disease is trying to teach us, as individuals or the world, then we will continue to create the conditions to promote them.

A truth lies at the true structure of all disease and the discovery of that truth will speed the development of its cure. The manifestation of fear and/or anger over a cancer which, as does fear and anger, eats away our being. A learning of oneness, as opposed to separateness, will assist in alleviating the need for diseases such as AIDS, leprosy, smallpox, sickle cell anemia and other race or group manifestations.

A recognition of our existence within the heart of God will allow us the ability to peacefully allow our physical being to be released to the creator. Through mastered awareness we can allow the physical to fall away when we have completed our life experience.

When we can quickly learn the truth of a disease we will stop giving it power it over us. We will rise to the experience and do what has to be done when they outlive predictions or return to a state of health. This return may be assisted in many ways but it must always be driven by the will; the will to change, to love, to live. Mother Teresa never questioned why a person was ill, she simply offered them love and the opportunity to die with dignity.

When we come to a recognition of the power of the will to bring ourselves back to the creator as our source we will find that it will no longer be necessary to continue to empower disease. We will empower balance and health, light and life, and share that expression of love with all of creation.

Ni-mahn

Energy System

PRIMARY ACTIVE ENERGY: Illumination

RESONATES TO THE MUSICAL NOTE: E

BALANCING COLOR: Orange

PRIMARY BALANCING ESSENTIAL OIL: *Ravensara Aromatica*

LOCATION: Navel

OTHER NAMES: Navel chakra

BALANCED CHARACTERISTICS:

- Releases the need for conformity
- Renews independence of spirit
- Opens the self to new social experiences
- Drives us to change our life where necessary
- Calls us to assess our role in life and our place in the world
- Gives us the ability to recognize God in our fellow beings
- Returns us to the awareness of the interrelation of our actions and conditions in the world
- Pushes us out of our self constructed boundaries and into freedom of expression

BODY SYSTEM

DIGESTIVE SYSTEM: The digestive system is concerned with the breakdown, digestion, and absorption of food as well as the passing of the unused portions. It begins in the mouth, continues to the abdomen and opens again at the anus. The liver, pancreas, and gall bladder are also glands associated with the digestive system.

Digestion begins as food is softened and partially digested by saliva. The stomach begins the chemical aspect of digestion and passes the food on into the small intestines, where more mechanical and enzymatic digestion continues. Bile, which assists in the breakdown of fats, is produced by the liver, stored in the gall bladder and is secreted into the duodenum as the next step in the process.

The next phase involves the large intestine where minerals and water are absorbed. In the final phase, unabsorbed and undigested material passes through the rectum for discharge.

INDICATORS OF IMBALANCE

With Ni-mahn out of balance, you find that you are unable to take in and fully absorb the fullness of life. You become limited to others' perception of what life should be. The stomach becomes irritated and the nutrients from food are not absorbed into the body. The spirit then becomes dampened and unable to enjoy the uniqueness of your life experience.

PRECEPT

This precept strives to bring about a balance of polarity on the earth and within individuals. It proposes that the earth and those who inhabit it, believe, that which was and has been, can no longer be. Knowledge must be developed to change the polarity of thinking which will in turn align the energy of the earth.

We must begin to recognize all of creation within ourselves. We need to be capable of seeing all races, genders, ages, sexual orientations, mental, physical and emotional functioning and species as a part of our being. To accomplish this, we must first put aside our fear of what we do not understand.

We need to understand that without darkness we would not recognize light. Without limitation we would not recognize freedom. Without the elders we would have no experience of youth. Without female there would be no male. Without homosexuality there would be no knowledge of heterosexuality. Without the plants and animals we would not be. Without love and compassion there would be no tomorrow.

Releasing our fears and bigotry is the beginning of realizing how we are complete. To recognize that our planet is in no way superior to another is to know that it is complete and exactly appropriate for our species. Often we feel that we have freed ourselves from the poison of bigotry when we no longer act superior to another. Seldom are we aware that the person we feel the most sympathy for, since they are not like us, is the very same person that we have the most to learn from.

Instead of trying to understand another, perhaps we should seek to find that part of ourselves which fears. If our acts of helping another and philanthropy are based in offering them the opportunity to be their very best, then they are truly acts of love. If acts are done so they can change their incorrect existence and become what we think is right, then we are in error and practicing bigotry. We must recognize their perfection in whatever they ultimately attain.

As we are polarized beings, so is all of creation. As we bring our polarity into balance through a oneness of light, the earth will be aligned with that awareness. An awareness that the changing of the magnetic polarity of the face of the earth does not require a physical readjusting of the earth in the heavens. It requires a spiritual repositioning of our intent. We must come to a realization of the balance and blending of earth and ourselves and bring into harmony all within it.

BAY-LARH

ENERGY SYSTEM

PRIMARY ACTIVE ENERGY: Awakening

RESONATES TO THE MUSICAL NOTE: F

BALANCING COLOR: Green

PRIMARY BALANCING ESSENTIAL OIL: *Anethum Graveolens*

LOCATION: Approximately 3 finger widths above the navel

OTHER NAMES: Solar Plexus chakra

BALANCED CHARACTERISTICS:

- Lifts you from limitation
- Renews freedom of the soul
- Creates empathy for others
- Develops understanding and compassion
- Allows us to feel good about who we are
- Enables a positive outlook in the midst of chaos
- Reacts to information from others and its application
- Stimulates choices that create positive results for the self and others

PERIPHERAL NERVOUS SYSTEM: The peripheral nervous system connects all the various parts of the body with the brain and spinal cord. The peripheral nervous system also includes the visceral of autonomic nervous system that is involved in our fight or flight responses. The groupings of these nerves are: the cranial nerves of the head, the spinal nerves, the cervical nerves to the neck, the nerves to the upper limbs, the nerves to the lower limbs, and the nerves to the dermatomes or areas of the skin.

The cranial nerves are receptors involved primarily in receiving four of the five physical senses. The olfactory receptors in the roof and walls of the nasal cavity are smell-sensitive. The visual receptors in the retina of the eye are light-sensitive. The receptors in the tongue are taste-sensitive. The receptors in the ear are sound-sensitive and sensitive to balance and movement of the head.

Spinal nerves originate from nerve roots that come directly off the spinal cord. There are 31 pairs of spinal nerves that enable the body to sense and move. Irritation or damage to these nerves can result in limited movement, numbness, and possible paralysis.

INDICATORS OF IMBALANCE

Just as when the peripheral nervous system is damaged or impaired, when Baylarh is out of balance you find the expression of your true self becomes paralyzed and unable to sense opportunity. You may experience back and leg pain and limited mobility, just as the freedom of the soul being suppressed limits your soul's growth.

PRECEPT

How many possibilities are there for a room in color, floor covering, ceiling and lighting? How many people are there? There are at least that many possibilities.

So then each person is aligned with one of those possibilities.

When all of the possibilities are brought together to a point of blending, they arrive at a point of harmony. Just as the universes have unlimited potential, these are reflected in you. So now you can discover the way that the precepts effect the world in general. All people must learn one of the most serious experiences that we have on this earth. We must become one with the energy of mercy and grace.

Grace is achieved through learning mercy and forgiveness. Forgiveness of the self and thereby of all creation brings about an energy of mercy upon the earth. This energy then leads us to grace. Grace is the expression of the soul which is unlimited by the illusions of the earthly experience.

The world has not yet achieved the ability to exist in the energy of grace. Until such time as all can act only from a point of love, grace cannot abound. For as long as one harms another, love does not rule the heart of all creation.

Then comes mercy. Mercy is the sharing of unconditional love. When you show mercy upon another you are practicing unconditional love.

Grace is like a big umbrella that covers you when you go out into the rain. Grace is the shielding from everything that falls around you. The rain is the shadows and grace is the umbrella that keeps it from you. Grace is the light which shines around you, becomes one with you and reflects the promise of the rainbow. Grace is unconditional. Grace does not forgive, it forgets.

Hol-mahn

Energy System

PRIMARY ACTIVE ENERGY: Integration

RESONATES TO THE MUSICAL NOTE: F#

BALANCING COLOR: Pink

PRIMARY BALANCING ESSENTIAL OIL: *Nardostachys Jatamansi*

LOCATION: Heart

OTHER NAMES: Heart chakra

BALANCED CHARACTERISTICS:

- Connects with the Goddess of creation and nurtures personal growth
- Renews expression of love through thought, word, and deed
- Recognizes the reflection of love
- Brings forth action to challenge injustice
- Forgives the self and others for clouded judgment and choices
- Recognizes positive potential in all life
- Guides physical actions and mental choices toward positive growth
- Rewards choices with a sense of peace
- Creates harmony
- Recognizes the rejection of love in others and honors it without expectation
- Gives freely of love without concern of validation
- Does not require acknowledgment or acceptance outside the self
- Drives the self to grow and learn

CARDIOVASCULAR SYSTEM: The cardiovascular system consists of the heart, arteries and veins.

Circulation of the blood begins with the heart. Blood is pumped from the heart into the arteries and returns to the heart through the veins.

The heart is the pump of the vascular system and contains four chambers. The two chambers on the right make up the pulmonary heart and the two chambers on the left make up the systemic heart.

The beating of the heart continues without benefit of conscious thought and continues to pump life-giving blood throughout the body. As blood circulates it seeks the path of least resistance. Blocked arteries cause the flow of blood to become limited to areas of the body and can result in stroke and death.

INDICATORS OF IMBALANCE

When Hol-mahn is out of balance, arteries may become blocked and love eludes you. You may find yourself becoming critical not only of others but intensely critical of yourself. You begin to forget the forgiving aspect of your ability. The flow of the creative life can become as constricted as the actual flow of the life force within the body.

PRECEPT

Judgment. A time that we fear, and a place where we exist. We are instructed to "Judge not that you be not judged." If all of creation can focus itself upon the one commandment to "Love one another as I have loved you," then we will indeed comply with the long standing Ten Commandments of the Old Testament.

If we have love for ourselves we will not harm ourselves through harming another. Our focus will remain on maintaining balance within ourselves. We will not want to steal, kill, lie, act jealously, or take what is our neighbor's. We will recognize each other in the true light of love and not inflict darkness toward another's light.

In this perfect existence there would be no need for judgment but the human race has not arrived at that point. Therefore, we stand in judgment of each other and most detrimentally ourselves. We still maintain a separateness from each other and measure other's deeds and accomplishments by our own. We are quick to condemn the actions of another but slow to realize that same act in ourselves. We judge others and ourselves and thereby create the need to forgive.

When we can come to the awareness that we can forgive, we can truly reflect this wisdom to others. When we can forgive ourselves for allowing others actions and deeds to release an expression, then we assist that person to the pursuit of light. Then we can become aware of what we see in ourselves and forgive that, not them for the anger. To forgive completely is to not allow the emotion to arise again.

If there were no greed, there would be no hunger. If there were no divisions of equality, there would be no lust. If there were no need for judgment, we would exist in full light and measurement would disappear.

TOL-MAHR

ENERGY SYSTEM

PRIMARY ACTIVE ENERGY: Awakening

RESONATES TO THE MUSICAL NOTE: G

BALANCING COLOR: Blue

PRIMARY BALANCING ESSENTIAL OIL: *Mentha Spicata*

LOCATION: Throat, over the thyroid

OTHER NAMES: Throat chakra

BALANCED CHARACTERISTICS:

- Calls forth your will into positive choices
- Renews the power of your spoken word
- Awakens the ability to effectively communicate to others
- Brings about leadership intelligence
- Removes fear of speaking forth and recognizes the validity of others' words
- Empowers the choosing of appropriate timing and energy to accomplish desired results
- Chooses words that build instead of destroy
- Guides the choice of expression into paths that resolve problems
- Controls the use of personal will over the choices of others
- Recognizes truth in all of creation and directs its simple use in all actions
- Begins the birth of manifestation into physical existence
- Refocuses the priorities to Divine will over the will of the ego

ENDOCRINE SYSTEM: The endocrine system consists of glands that secrete hormones into the tissue fluids and blood that affects the function of multiple areas of the body. The system consists primarily of the pituitary, pineal, thyroid, parathyroid, thymus, adrenals, and pancreas.

Hormones affect our height and build, sexual activity, mental sharpness, ability to respond to stress and more. There is not a single body cell whose activity is not in some way affected by hormones secreted by the endocrine system.

The thyroid, located at the base of the neck on both sides of the windpipe, regulates the rate of chemical processes in the body. Hormonal secretions of the pituitary gland regulate the activity of the thyroid. The thyroid is one of the master glands and if it produces either too much or too little thyroxin, serious life-threatening disorders may result.

Hormones regulate many, perhaps all of the vital body processes. The hormone, adrenaline, is secreted when the body is under stress and is carried to all parts of the body enabling it to respond with tremendous strength and unusual ability. When the situation has passed, adrenaline is broken down chemically and disposed of by the liver.

INDICATORS OF IMBALANCE

Just as the endocrine system can call forth amazing power from the body, Tol-mahr calls forth the power of the will. When Tol-mahr is out of balance, you find yourself trapped in situations which limit your freedom. You are dominated by other's choices until you begin to speak your truth and regain the use of your will. The body often responds to your silence with hyper or hypo activity of the thyroid causing hormonal imbalance. Tol-mahr imbalance sends you spiraling into a current; subject to the will of the tides instead of firmly in control of your life directed by your will verbalized into action.

Your next precept brings you into an aspect of The Trinity. As you become one with Father, Son and Spirit, you must now activate recreative power. You must realize the potential of the Father/Mother, Son/ Daughter and Spirit/Self and come into balance with it. For only then will you be capable of accepting the responsibility that comes with creating.

The Trinity exists as The Father, which is your origin, The Sun, which is your sustenance and The Spirit, which is your continuance. Therefore, when you proclaim something in the name of The Father, The Son and The Holy Spirit, all of your being is in complete balance and harmony.

We, as a race, find much comfort in placing blame. All natural disasters are an act of God. When bad things happen, something evil causes it and lures good people into bad behavior. When an earthquake occurs shortly after the testing of a nuclear bomb, it is a "natural disaster." When the Greenhouse Effect threatens the very existence of all life, we search for an explanation but don't look in the mirror or modify our choices. It is the fault of something beyond us. Not the result of choices within us.

To find The Trinity becoming as one, balanced and aligned, we must understand ourselves as a reflection of God. We must know the part of God that dwells within us and the part of us that dwells within God. To discover this you must take The Trinity aspect of yourself, bring it into balance, and express it outward. You must put aside the limitation of stereotyped behavior and recognize the fullness of your own being. You must take responsibility for your choices and actions. Through separateness, fear is born. Through wholeness, fear is absolved by love.

Speaking from within, where we realize the potential of our choices, we begin to become responsible beings. A truly aligned being utilizes the power of their words for positive creative manifestation. Words spoken from a place of anger create a response of anger or destruction. Words spoken with fear elicit actions of fear. When we activate responsibility for our words, we begin to access the power of change. Through our words we manifest the ability to lift up or tear down another individual and our world.

Allowing the will to be expressed only from a point of balance creates positive change. This expression begins within the self. If an individual cannot recognize the beauty and potential of their own spirit, they cannot create beauty around themselves. This person continues to place the source of results outside of their choices and cannot create change.

The creative use of will is based in a recognition of cause and effect. This recognition guides the individual to wise choices and the joy found in positive results.

CAL-MAHR

ENERGY SYSTEM

PRIMARY ACTIVE ENERGY: Illumination

RESONATES TO THE MUSICAL NOTE: G#

BALANCING COLOR: White

PRIMARY BALANCING ESSENTIAL OIL: *Commiphora Myrrha*

LOCATION: Behind the neck between the top of the shoulders and base of the skull

OTHER NAMES: Causal chakra

BALANCED CHARACTERISTICS:

- Renews mind, body, spirit connection
- Blends physical will with an understanding of your higher purpose
- Allows us to see the larger picture for our life
- Brings an active awareness of a higher or more perfect aspect of ourselves existing within us
- Recognizes which choices will allow us to bring our potential into being
- Remains clear and focused no matter the lessons, noise, or confusion of the world
- Awakens the ability to calm the mind and be receptive to the gentle guidance of spirit
- Blends the power of Divine Law into our choices
- Holds the clarity of inspiration safe from mental pollution

RESPIRATORY SYSTEM: One of the first independent functions of our body when separated from our mother's womb is to breathe. This function is possible due to the respiratory system.

The respiratory system consists primarily of the nasal cavity, pharynx, larynx, trachea, bronchi, bronchial tree, lungs and diaphragm. Air is pulled into the lungs primarily by the force of the diaphragm. Once in the lungs the oxygen is absorbed by the blood.

When the nasal cavities are blocked, pressure builds and creates extreme pain. Clear sinus passages lighten the skull and add timbre to the voice.

The lungs are the primary areas where the outside world has the easiest access to the interior cavities of the body.

Indicators of Imbalance

Without oxygen the mind becomes clouded and the body cannot function. When oxygen begins to flow again, the mind clears and the body is renewed. When Cal-mahr is out of balance we become separated from our life force and cannot continue with renewed spirit. Separation causes us to loose the enthusiasm and energy to continue life. We begin to fall subject to infections and diseases that limit our ability to take in the very breath of life.

Precept

After allowing fear to control the world, the people of the earth have turned God into a fearful thing. This thinking cannot manifest love upon the earth. God is believed to be intolerant of violence, yet our children are still filled with rage and act it out on other children. We have not taught our children that all things are equal and are to be respected.

The teaching of God as vengeful and wrathful has not eliminated hatred, famine and disease. It has allowed the people of the Earth to take action as enforcers of that wrath and vengeance to segregate, condemn and apply justice by their own individual acts.

Therefore, people need to create an image which reflects the existence of spirit, love, respect for all life, and healing as the heart of God. That is needed for the Earth to heal. People have shown that they cannot heal the Earth themselves. They cannot clean the air of pollutants, purify and give life to lakes or repair the very atmosphere that the creations of their higher intelligence have destroyed. They must recognize and reawaken themselves to that God of Love that is the very essence of their being. By the creation of a fearful, vengeful, wrathful God the people of the Earth have called that very part of themselves to come forth.

We are taught that we must strive to become like God. Our every thought, word or deed should be focused upon the principle that God is watching everything we do. If we then teach our children of a God of anger and vengeance, how then can we expect their behavior to reflect anything less.

If we continue to teach of a God that destroys, requires the sacrifice of lambs, brings plagues, and all forms of wrath upon the Earth how can we produce a generation that believes in the ability of love to heal? What do we expect our children and the masses to become when this is our standard? When we replace the concept of God based in fear with the emphasis to "make love our aim," (I Corinthians 14:1) we can begin again.

We, as a race, have created anger, hatred, bigotry and fear as the face of God. We teach through threat instead of emphasizing the consequence of choices.

We have proven that anger, wrath and vengeance cannot heal, for we have created a world in war and chaos. Now we must unite, through love, to begin to recreate the Earth. To recognize the loving, comforting, caring, forgiving nature of The Creator. This will unveil a being of radiant light that is the heart of God.

This can produce a generation united through the heart, mind and soul. United through the embodiment of the Love of God. You can be as one light, as one energy, united through your hearts, beginning with each other. You must stand with each other with no awareness of division. Only when we can stand with each other united can you practice these things.

VI-MAHN

ENERGY SYSTEM

PRIMARY ACTIVE ENERGY: Integration

RESONATES TO THE MUSICAL NOTE: A

BALANCING COLOR: Indigo

PRIMARY BALANCING ESSENTIAL OIL: *Jasminum Officianle*

LOCATION: Center of brow

OTHER NAMES: Third eye chakra

BALANCED CHARACTERISTICS:

- Maintains connection with Divine Purpose
- Renews clarity of vision toward the greater good
- Sharpens intuitive intelligence
- Helps to manifest our dreams by maintaining our focus
- Reveals clearest path of action
- Recognizes the Divine purpose in all physical action, choice and experience
- Retains knowledge of how the life experience is unfolding and integrates it into our choices
- Allows us to see ourselves in others actions
- Reveals the potential consequences of our choices enabling educated decisions

MUSCULAR SYSTEM: The muscular system consists of muscles that move the body, the face and other structures giving form to the body. This system also includes the cardiac muscle of the heart walls.

Painless movement is possible with integrated and harmonious muscle functioning; no muscle acts alone in the movement of a joint.

The muscular system enables movement. Voluntary muscles respond to conscious control but also can act involuntarily as in a reflex action.

Cardiac muscles form the heart. The beating of the heart is maintained by the cardiac pacemaker which is a small piece of tissue made up of nerve and muscle cells located in the wall of the right auricle.

Muscles become larger and stronger with use. Unused muscles atrophy or shrivel away. These factors indicate the importance of movement and exercise, for without them you loose muscle functioning. Any movement inside the body as well as movement of the body as a whole is accomplished by the muscles.

INDICATORS OF IMBALANCE

Without the muscles the body is unable to move. When Vi-mahn is out of balance, your forward movement is inhibited. With the clarity of vision of your Divine Purpose, you are able to move forward in harmony instead of reacting in an involuntary or reflex manner. With Vi-mahn out of balance, you find yourself in a constant state of putting out fires instead of stepping forth with assured action. Heart pains and arrhythmia may begin to manifest.

PRECEPT

This precept is based upon an understanding of each individual's own energy and that everyone does operate with Essential energy centers. The Earth has progressed to a point where people must recognize the twelve-fold aspect of their energy flow.

There is a twelve-fold energy field within each person that has not been brought into total activation. People must now begin to work with this twelve-fold flow of energy. They must cease to place their existence totally within the realm of the Earth and what they feel they have created upon it. They must begin to place their vision upon the alignment with the power available. As it is when the self is centered in the heart of creation, the heart of God.

The awakening of these Essential energy points brings with it a perception. Everyone must expand their vision and increase the power within to unfold all flows of creative energy. In bringing this twelve-fold energy flow into yourself, you will open avenues that present the fullness of that true self and bring it into a trinity. This trinity reflects the true God The Father, Son and Spirit that is now the self as a product of creation. This realized self is that light that is external to all creation and internal to the self.

The Earth has existed in the sevenfold reality of The Father and Son. It now becomes the task to open the heart and mind to the Spirit that was promised.

Many of the years spent upon this Earth have been spent in a limited understanding. By opening to the twelve-fold potential, we allow ourselves to be filled and fully awakened to the existence of Spirit.

If we utilize the example of the New Jerusalem, as depicted in Revelation 21 and 22, we will receive an understanding that each of the twelve gates spoken of has a base in Spirit. This Spirit is illustrated through the characteristics of the disciples, the awareness of the joining of the races through the twelve tribes of Israel, the angelic realm, the stones of the Earth and an alignment with our own being. The awakening of these twelve gates, or energy centers of the self, opens us to the awareness of the temple of God that exists within each of us. This awakening brings one to the point of existence in the full light of love, where "darkness no longer dwells." The confusion of our own mental minds gives way to the peace of the Spirit of Truth. In this temple there is "no need for a candle," for we can stand as in-lightened beings in our full illumination.

The Earth has become familiarized with the angelic realm and embraced it as a saving grace. It has personalized angels on television, in the movies, and through all forms of fashion and marketing. Now it is time to move into a broader experience and listen and learn as spirit shares the wisdom of the ages. Wisdom that allows us to be with them today in paradise.

Hal-rai

Energy System

PRIMARY ACTIVE ENERGY: Illumination

RESONATES TO THE MUSICAL NOTE: B flat

BALANCING COLOR: Purple

PRIMARY BALANCING ESSENTIAL OIL: *Larus Nobilis*

LOCATION: Top of head

OTHER NAMES: Crown chakra

BALANCED CHARACTERISTICS:

- Reclaims self mastery
- Renews commitment of spirit
- Clarifies what you desire
- Keeps you on track toward goals and dreams
- Defines the path of God into personal choice
- Integrates wisdom untainted by ego into your actions
- Incorporates the ability to recognize the importance of your existence in the balance of all creation
- Guides the simplest of choices to maintain positive results
- Reminds us of our responsibility for all choices and shows us potential results

THE SKIN (INTEGUMENTARY) SYSTEM: The skin consists of two layers; the epidermis and the dermas, and is the largest organ of the human body. The skin is the body's protective coat. It is our umbrella, sunshade, cooling system and still responds to the lightest touch, temperature change and pain. It is constantly in a state of regeneration and repair.

The nails are constantly growing away from the body and are plates of compacted, highly keratinized cells.

The dermas supports arteries, veins, lymphatic capillaries, nerves and sensory receptors. Sweat glands are located in the deep dermas. The glandular cells at the base and close to capillaries, produce sweat, which is primarily salt water with small amounts of urea and other molecules. The hypothalamus instigates sweating to assist the body in cooling through evaporation.

The skin, just like ourselves, is in a constant state of change. It is our early warning system to conditions and elements of the Earth that require response or adjustment from other aspects of the body. The skin maintains focus of the body and keeps all essential components contained in one covering, protecting the delicate structures within.

INDICATORS OF IMBALANCE

When Hal-rai is out of balance, we become easily deterred from the commitment to mastering the self and our spiritual path. We are subject to scrapes and bruises from the outer world. We are constantly bounced from one direction to another. This can remove our focus from our desired direction of growth. These scrapes and bruises require the attention of our energy, just as a cut or bruise to the skin focuses all of our attention to the area injured. We freeze where we are and the injured area becomes master of our actions. When we allow others' words and deeds to divert our focus and energy, we give them mastery over our path of action and cease to control our own destiny.

The foundation of the energy that this age will be based in is the energy of Healing and Truth. The healing of all creation and the clearest and highest truth. Truth has begun its consumption of falsity even through the exposing of those we place in power over us and those we trust to produce food and other products for consumption. Healing has begun its process of power over death by the uniting of diversified hearts in the deaths of Princess Diana and Mother Teresa, giving understanding to what they stood for.

Now, when you enter into an age of achieving higher truth and receiving the energy of healing, you enter into what some may call the age of Mastery. In order to achieve the full light of truth and healing, you must first master the only thing you can truly master, the self. This is your first and foremost priority. Upon that foundation this precept is built. You must come to a point where you can allow truth to burn away falsity within yourself and still remain standing and be sustained.

In this mastery of the self you become an immovable and unshakable force upon the Earth. You realize that you may not be doing what everyone else is doing but you continue on. Those unquenchable thirsts of your soul for truth, healing, light and love may not be what the world is supplying but it is what it seeks.

When you come to the point where you are immovable and unshakable, it does not mean that you are not open to new ideas and cannot change as energy changes. It does not mean that you are set in your ways and will not see new possibilities. It means that you become, within yourself, an energy that cannot be placed into fear, doubt or guilt. All of these things are darkened emotions that cloud the skies of light.

This is a difficult experience. This is a difficult precept. What you are coming into is an energy within you that, no matter what occurs around you, it does not remove you from your path of spiritual discovery. Just because you are born under a certain astrological sign or reared in a certain environment, you do not have to accept that you have no ability to change. You recognize the strength of truth and healing within yourself and see all things around you as an opportunity to strengthen and expand the self.

If you feel that you are beautiful as a blond and another begins to tell dumb blonde jokes, you do not allow the emotion to rise to the point of control through retaliation. You recognize that they exist in the energy of their own progression and allow them to travel that path. Just as Jesus spoke of "turning the other cheek," he recognized the need to address another perspective. A blow to your being is to be turned to light. The act must be addressed, brought to the other's attention as a negative, and reversed. A negative aspect is to be turned to a positive outcome. The ability to control the self will redirect the energy of the world.

HAL-MARD

ENERGY SYSTEM

PRIMARY ACTIVE ENERGY: Illumination

RESONATES TO THE MUSICAL NOTE: B

BALANCING COLOR: Silver/Gray

PRIMARY BALANCING ESSENTIAL OIL: Hyssop

LOCATION: six inches above the head

OTHER NAMES: Soul Star

BALANCED CHARACTERISTICS:

- Opens the door to Divine inspiration
- Renews life-changing ability
- Key to mastery of soul's purpose
- Allows you to recognize your soul's purpose in daily life
- Reveals the unity of spirit of all aspects of creation
- Discloses how all of creation will contribute to your choices that bring about positive change
- Allows the actions to become focused on the good of the whole
- Illumines where individual choice reflects in world events and conditions
- Removes the illusion of petty distractions and increases the awareness of guided opportunities
- Frees us to recognize and utilize the gifts available throughout all of creation

CENTRAL NERVOUS SYSTEM: The Central Nervous System consists primarily of the brain, thalamus, hypothalamus, pineal gland, and spinal cord. The brain consists of four major lobes. 1) The frontal which is concerned with intellectual functions including reasoning, and abstract thinking, aggression, sexual behavior, smell, speech, and voluntary movement. 2) The parietal lobe which is concerned with body sensory awareness, taste, language, abstract reasoning, and body imaging. 3) The temporal lobe which is concerned with the formation of emotions, interpretation of language, hearing, and a major memory processing area. 4) The occipital lobe which receives, interprets, and discriminates visual stimulation.

The thalamus integrates sensory experiences and input resulting in appropriate motor and emotional responses. The pineal gland produces melatonin which is key to regulating our body cycles relating to night and day. The hypothalamus is concerned with emotional behavior. The spinal cord is the brain's channel for communication with the rest of the body and the path for the body-mind connection.

INDICATORS OF IMBALANCE

When Hal-mard is out of balance, you have difficulty making clear choices toward change that empowers your soul. The brain cannot receive information and make choices appropriately without its connection to the body via the spinal cord. We cannot make empowering choices to change as appropriate without our connection to divine inspiration. Just as the thalamus maintains the body's conscious awareness, Hal-mard maintains our awareness of divine inspiration. With Hal-mard out of balance our thoughts become clouded and our judgment impaired. We may begin to have difficulty seeing what is truly there physically, mentally, and emotionally. Difficulties with depth perception may begin to manifest.

The inability to believe or trust in your ability or alignment with the mind of God comes from a feeling of separateness. Feeling that you are not worthy of being a part of God.

We seek union with groups of people in an attempt to remind us that we are part of a bigger whole. We are not sure what it is we are looking for. Many times as we join clubs, churches or groups, we understand the need for associating with others as filling that void of belonging. Possibly in this act we are seeking a remembrance of the union of spirit that we all have through the mind of God.

The alignment with that is the manner in which we may pursue reunion. We lose sight of: "For by one Spirit we were all baptized into one body -Jews or Greeks, slaves or free -and all were made to drink of one Spirit" (I Corinthians 12:13). Separateness is not an act of the mind of God for through Light we are united, "Now you are the body of Christ and individually members of it" (I Corinthians 12:27). So then separateness is an act of our minds and affects all life.

Communion with Spirit is an absolute necessity as we enter into this age. Jesus illustrated with the communion he shared with the disciples. You have communion in remembrance of the union you have with the mind of God. You continue this communion so that you might not fear for the words that you would speak but allow yourself to receive the words through the Spirit. For we seek reunion with the love that we left within the heart of God and can only achieve it through realigning with the mind of God. Remember your body, remember your blood, remember your life, your true life which exists within the heart and mind of God. It is a gathering of love and light which is within all of creation.

When we were all one energy, united in the purpose of creation as illustrated in Genesis, we knew in that moment that we contained all things. In order to give life to an Earth and all things upon it we must be a part of that which is born.

DNA testing quickly proves relationship on a physical level, but the miracle of a beating heart and the breath of life lends credence to a relationship on another.

Even when we can, through our hearts, recognize all creation as one energy, we have not yet learned to recognize all things within ourselves or ourselves in all things. If we believe that God created the heavens and the Earth and all things thereon, then it must be that all creation, including ourselves, is born of God. If we are born of God, at some moment we as well as all creation, must have been a part of God. If so, then it must follow that we are a part of God.

In order to become individualized portions we then must have separated from God. Before that separation, when we were a unified energy of God, we then too knew all things. We knew that we would strive to become separate beings. We knew that we would lose our awareness of God. We knew that we would create fear and hatred. We knew that we would create the capability to destroy all of creation. We accessed the unified knowledge of all things in order to create the ability to alienate all things. We easily call upon the source of all knowing to provide ways to forget it all.

In that moment when we were unified in one energy, we knew that we were all things but we could not recognize that we were all things. Just as we now consider our body as one thing complete in itself, we often times cannot consider all of its parts. The only time we give attention to an individual part of our body is when it is not in balance or as perfect as we would wish it to be. Similarly, we do not give to all of creation our attention until it has reached a point of imbalance. Perhaps, just as with our body, if we would recognize the whole of it as existing in parts and strive to maintain the balance of the whole we would not allow disease or wars to begin. We would perceive unrest, pain and disharmony before it grew to a point of bringing chaos within us.

In the time of dividing from the whole to become individualized beings, we established within ourselves the feeling of inadequacy. The feeling of the inability to accomplish the tasks we were preparing to do. The feeling of only being a little part. This feeling began within us the need to accomplish "something" in our lives, to be special, to be better, to be important. The need to be better then established a foundation for the fear that we were not good enough and measurement fell into place. We lost sight of the possibility that each part of the whole has a specific part to play out to achieve the culmination of the task and created the need to do it all alone or be a failure. We ceased to recognize how each part is equal. We fail to look at the aspect that if there were no hungry or poor, there would be no need for philanthropy. If there were no alcoholics there would be no need for a "Twelve-Step Program" that offers hope to many.

"If the whole body were an eye, where would be the hearing? If the whole body were an ear, where would be the sense of smell? But as it is, God arranged the organs in the body, each one of them as he chose. If all were a single organ, where would the body be? As it is, there are many parts, yet one body" (I Corinthians 12:17 -19).

To understand how we created this fear of separateness let us consider a simple task. At work you and a partner have always moved an object together, never have you attempted it alone. Then comes the day when your partner does not show up in time to move the object and it has to be done immediately. Your first thought, before you even attempt, most probably would be that you cannot move it alone. You have always done it with your partner. You would create the fear before you even began the attempt because you failed to recognize how much you are a part of the whole. You have access to all that is available within it. You may even hesitate to ask another to assist you because you would be fearful that they were not as capable as your partner or willing to work with you on your menial task. You would activate that same feeling of separation from the whole which is instilled within you from the point of your individualization from the whole, or mind of God. It has always been a collective awareness, the whole, the mind of God, but we have created a separateness or distanced ourselves from that knowing. That separation from the whole created the need for an awareness of God as an individualized, personalized being. In our feelings of inadequacy, we therefore created a superior God with standards that continue to present to us goals which we feel unable to attain. We created a need for assistance and felt that it was inappropriate to ask another person for they are as separate and distanced from God as ourselves. If they are human, they too are inadequate. Then come those few that we recognize as special, unique, brilliant and able to perform things that we could only dream of. These are the souls who can so quickly touch that mind of God and bring it into a physical reality. These individuals seek alignment with that collective awareness and apply it to their daily living. They serve the whole and accept all of creation as a part of the same. They "walk their talk." When someone does align with the mind of God and achieve their full potential, we canonize them and place them above the possibility of ourselves, instead of looking to their example and striving for the same.

If we are a part of that whole, how then do we align with the potential and expansion that it has to offer us? This is how The Age of Spirit serves us as we serve its dawning. If you have a need there is nothing that is not available to you. This is the foundation of The Age of Spirit. That you would know, "With men this is impossible, but with God all things are possible." (Matthew 19:26)

When all of life began, all of creation was whole in that awareness and part of that creative process, then the part of us that remains as a part of God awaits our remembrance. If a part of everything in creation exists there in that same moment, then the part of us that remains a part of God is unified in spirit with everything. So then to align with the mind of God we must make ourselves quiet and remember that part of us remains a part of God. Therefore, a part of God remains in us. We must find that part of ourselves, which is unconditional in love and awaken it so that we are then aware of our connection with all of creation. Once this awareness is established, we can more readily open our hearts and minds to the spirit of creation.

Awakening to the mind of God is much likened to walking into a shopping mall. You walk into the mall alone with an objective. Once you are in the building, you become part of a larger group of shoppers. You are aware of people, what they are wearing, what they say to you and others, if they carry a lot of baggage, if they appear lonely, if they appear happy. Those things and more then become a part of your day. You allow yourself to become one with everything around you. If you meet a sales clerk having a bad day or you have kind and efficient service your attitude is affected. You align with the energy of your experience. You may remember the lonely face of an elderly person, the frightened face of a lost child, or the friendly smile or nod. You feel a part of their experience. If you are looking for something, and you're not sure exactly where it is or what it is called, you ask for assistance. When you are directed to what you need or you find it on your own, you return home with all that you needed.

And so it is with the mind of God. All that you desire and can imagine awaits you. And all you must do to obtain it is seek it.

STEPS IN AWAKENING TO THE MIND OF GOD

- You walk in, alone with an objective.
- You become part of a larger group.
- You allow yourself to become one with everything around you.
- You align with the energy of your experience.
- You feel a part of everyone's experience.
- You ask for assistance.
- You return home with all that you needed.

Hal-lái

Energy System

PRIMARY ACTIVE ENERGY: Integration

RESONATES TO THE MUSICAL NOTE: C above middle C

BALANCING COLOR: Gold/Mustard

PRIMARY BALANCING ESSENTIAL OIL: Angelica

LOCATION: 12 inches above the head

OTHER NAMES: Stellar Gateway

BALANCED CHARACTERISTICS:

- Awakens the cellular memory
- Discloses the accumulated life experiences and their wisdom in the present
- Ultimate connection to the source of creation
- Allows you to recognize the effect of personal decisions on the whole of creation
- Guides your choices toward the greater good
- Blends spiritual realities into physical existence
- Enables us to maintain a continual link to all of creation
- Blends the oneness of our existence into the wholeness of God
- Activates communion with the past, present, and future and brings it fully into the moment

LYMPHATIC SYSTEM: The lymphatic system consists primarily of the thymus, spleen, red bone marrow, lymph nodes, tonsils, adenoids, and appendix. It is our primary guardian against disease. It empowers our natural and acquired immunity. The lymph node is the site of T-cell immune response. It is generally infected at a rapid rate by the human immunodeficiency virus (HIV), causing acquired immunodeficiency syndrome (AIDS), affecting most parts of the immune system at one point or another.

In the past, it was common practice to surgically remove the tonsils, adenoids and appendix. Currently, tonsils and adenoids are removed only for good cause, for they respond quickly to the presence of microorganisms by either alerting the T-cells or destroying them with antibodies. The primary function of the spleen is the production of antibodies, therefore, the absence of the spleen greatly reduces the capabilities of the immune system.

The lymphatic system has no pump such as the heart in the circulatory system to move the fluid through it. The lymphatic system is the anatomical component of the immune system and defends the body against the invasion of microorganisms as well as destroying cells or cell parts that are not inherent to the body.

INDICATORS OF IMBALANCE

When Hal-lái is out of balance you are more subject to infectious disease. You more strongly accept the beliefs of the people of the Earth than the truths of the Creator. Just as the immune system defends the body, connecting to the universal source of life defends the soul.

PRECEPT

With your final precept, you have the culmination of the All of All. Jesus revealed many secrets in his teachings but often they were too simple to understand.

We as a superior race feel that something must be difficult in order to be worth attaining. So then, to offer us an opportunity to feel that we discovered something and unraveled a great mystery, he spoke to us in parables.

The culmination of the All of All comes through the simple understanding of love. Jesus said to us, "I am the light of the world" (John 9:5). When we remember that God has revealed His name through the burning bush as "I Am," we then can recognize that God is the light of the world. Through the simple expression of light, all will unite as one.

Your final precept is the most simple of all, therefore, becoming the most difficult to understand. For it is a precept that you cannot hear nor say. It is a precept that you must walk, live and be. It is a precept that you become. It is a precept that you share through your existence, not with your words, but through your light. It can only serve and be served by you.

To say that all of the prophets passed away with the death of those in the Bible is to turn over responsibility of our lives to men who walked this Earth over two thousand years ago. This is a safe manner in which to conduct our lives, for with this surrender we cease to accept responsibility for a world of our own creation. In this thinking we release our destiny to a fate they envisioned. When we recognize the Essentials of our being and our active participation in creating a world controlled by fear, we come one step closer to understanding.

If we believe that God does indeed continue to speak through His prophets, then possibly we are ready to address a new understanding. To recognize the Essentials of our being to reclaim our ability to change within a world within change.

We stand at the threshold of the changing of an age. It is necessary that we prepare ourselves to usher in that energy of change. It is necessary for those who are working with wisdom to become aware and begin to utilize the Essentials of their being. It is imperative for those who seek understanding to have time to build their wholeness and employ the use of these foundations.

The development and reawakening of our awareness of the Essentials of our being does not require a commitment to any specific or organized religion. There is no one belief system that holds all guidance, direction and truth. There is only one direction; the seeking of truth and the acceptance of responsibility for our actions and ourselves that will lead us toward the enlightenment of our essential being. In acceptance of that responsibility, we come to recognize a power which exists to aid us in that search. Hopefully, we turn to our connection to that source. Whether we term it God, Higher Power, Creator, or whatever name we give it for our guidance in the awakening process.

Many who study the higher truths seek only the enlightenment of their own self. But, the age that this Earth is entering into requires that all who are upon that path share, through their example and existence, the wisdom they are acquiring. Upon this Earth, at this time, so we are called.

Many would say, send another If those disciples and apostles who learned from those teachings offered by Jesus had said the same there would be no basis of understanding from which this age is to be born. The story would not have been told.

If we do choose to serve the need of creation in the returning to wholeness, then we must awaken the Essentials of our being and bring them into balance. We must begin. Yes, there is required sacrifice. We are not required to be nailed to a cross, stoned to death, or beheaded. The sacrifices that are asked for to awaken the Essentials of your being are in your old thinking. They are in your perceptions of what you see as reality. You are asked to focus upon the Essentials of your being and carry that wisdom forth into your life so that others may know and be returned to wholeness.

As you gain strength, you will pass through many tests. Those who are fearful of the changes in understanding and gaining of wisdom, usually fear losing power over and control of the direction of Earth. These people act out their fear by challenging anyone who would offer hope to the people of the world through a path. They would attempt to convince you that you are wrong, that your truth is ludicrous or heresy.

But how ludicrous is it to believe that the reawakening of the Essentials of your being offers hope to a world of fear, hatred, and confusion? Is it any more sane to believe that the world may continue in the same manner it has and survive?

A visionary and administrator in the development of Pathway University School of Natural Healing, Dr. Wade's enthusiasm and expansion in the blending of Allopathic Medicine and Natural Healing has brought national recognition to this school.

Serving as a Noncommissioned Officer for over eight years in the Army, Dr. Wade completed training as a Hospital Medical Specialist and Field Medical Specialist. She expanded into the civilian world as a Certified Massage Therapist, Emergency Medical Technician and certified instructor for the State of Kentucky's Vocational Education in Emergency Medicine, CPR, and "First Responder," a program she was instrumental in developing for firefighters and law enforcement.

Majoring in Psychology at Indiana University Southeast and later Medical and Hospital Administration at University of Louisville. Dr. Wade began her studies into Healing in 1973. Her medical background and ongoing studies in Alternative Health led her to earn her Master Herbalist, Doctor of Naturopathy and Ph.D. in Spirituality.

An instructor for Pathway University, Dr. Wade also served as a consultant in Leavenworth, Indiana where she resided.

Notes

Notes

Notes